PRENTICE HALL
WRITING AND
GRAMMAR

Grammar Exercise Workbook

Grade Eleven

PEARSON
Prentice
Hall

Boston, Massachusetts,
Upper Saddle River, New Jersey

ISBN 0-13-361695-9

17 18 V039 16 15 14

Contents

Note: This workbook supports Chapters 17–27 (Part 2: Grammar, Usage, and Mechanics) of Prentice Hall *Writing and Grammar*.

Name _____ Date _____

 17.1 **Nouns • Practice 1**

Nouns A noun is the name of a person, place, or thing. Singular nouns name one person, place, or thing. Plural nouns name more than one. A compound noun is a noun that is made up of more than one word. A common noun names any one of a class of people, places, or things. A proper noun names a specific person, place, or thing.

Singular Nouns	shoe	knife
Plural Nouns	shoes	knives
Compound Nouns	mother-in-law	bridge table
Common Nouns	month	mountain
Proper Nouns	April	Appalachian Mountains

A concrete noun names something you can see, touch, taste, hear, or smell. An abstract noun names something you cannot perceive through your senses.

Concrete Nouns	Abstract Nouns
motorcycle	happiness
concert	intelligence
spaghetti	curiosity

▶ **Exercise 1** **Recognizing Nouns.** Underline each noun in the sentences below.

EXAMPLE: Her decision was to pack the biscuits in foil.

1. To our dismay, the escalator halted between floors.
2. Sally bought an encyclopedia on technology.
3. Can Amy get the cooperation of her classmates?
4. Ted is interested in the origin of words.
5. Halifax is the capital of Nova Scotia.
6. The surgeon predicted gradual improvement of her health.
7. First-class postage has almost doubled in this decade.
8. Mr. Reid disagreed with her decision on that issue.
9. A violent storm threatened the coast and the valley.
10. Jane made a jack-o'-lantern for the party on Saturday.

▶ **Exercise 2** **Identifying Concrete and Abstract Nouns.** Write *concrete* or *abstract* next to each noun.

EXAMPLE: fear _____*abstract*_____

1. dictionary _____
2. willingness _____
3. sailboat _____
4. statue _____
5. preparation _____
6. field _____
7. thermometer _____
8. arena _____
9. desperation _____
10. photocopy _____

11. democracy _____
12. hope _____
13. handbook _____
14. perfume _____
15. jealousy _____
16. witness _____
17. mortality _____
18. computer _____
19. conscience _____
20. orphanage _____

17.1 Nouns • Practice 2

▶ **Exercise 1**   **Identifying Types of Nouns.**   Write whether each noun (1) names a *person*, *place* or *thing*, (2) is *concrete* or *abstract*, (3) is *singular* or *plural*, (4) is *collective*, (5) is *compound*, and (6) is *common* or *proper*.

EXAMPLE: freedom _____ *(1) thing, (2) abstract, (3) singular, (4) not collective, (5) not compound, (6) common* _____

1. coat _____
2. editor-in-chief _____
3. Dallas _____
4. Julian Street _____
5. make-believe _____
6. joy _____
7. main-topsail _____
8. happiness _____
9. Ensign Alice Ross _____
10. velvet _____
11. wristwatches _____
12. wisdom _____
13. tablespoon _____
14. Lake Louise _____
15. flock _____

▶ **Exercise 2**   **Writing Sentences with Nouns.**   Write a sentence that includes the kind of noun indicated in parentheses.

EXAMPLE: (abstract, singular) _____ *Love is a powerful emotion.* _____

1. (concrete, singular)_____
2. (proper, plural)_____
3. (abstract, singular)_____
4. (common, plural)_____
5. (collective, singular)_____
6. (compound, plural)_____
7. (concrete, plural)_____
8. (proper, singular)_____
9. (abstract, plural)_____
10. (common, singular)_____
11. (collective, plural)_____
12. (compound, singular)_____
13. (concrete, singular)_____
14. (proper, plural)_____
15. (common, plural)_____

17.1 Pronouns • Practice 1

Pronouns A pronoun is a word used to take the place of a noun. The noun it substitutes for is called an antecedent.

PRONOUNS AND ANTECEDENTS
ANTECEDENT PRONOUN PRONOUN *Christopher* asked *his* teacher if *he* could leave early. PRONOUN   ANTECEDENT PRONOUN Is *that* the new football *player* about *whom* Jo told Jean?

Indefinite pronouns refer to nouns, often without specifying which ones. Some indefinite pronouns have antecedents, but many do not.

INDEFINITE PRONOUNS				
Singular			**Plural**	**Both**
another	everyone	no one	both	all
anybody	everybody	nothing	few	any
anyone	little	one	many	more
anything	much	other	others	most
each	neither	somebody	several	none
either	nobody	someone	some	

▷ **Exercise 1** **Recognizing Pronouns and Antecedents.** Underline the personal pronoun in each sentence and circle its antecedent.

EXAMPLE: Because of <u>her</u> cold, (Susan) could not attend.

1. Todd gave his class ring to Betsy.

2. Where will you stay in London, Phil?

3. With their oxygen running low, the divers signaled for help.

4. Jeff asked his father for the keys to the car.

5. Beethoven wrote his violin concerto in 1806.

6. When she finished the novel, Pam turned on the phonograph.

7. Maggie, have you outlined the research paper yet?

8. "I am going to Denver for Christmas," Pat told Derrick.

9. The congressman said that he would speak first.

10. The car in the driveway has its lights on.

▷ **Exercise 2** **Adding Indefinite Pronouns to Sentences.** Fill in each blank with an appropriate indefinite pronoun. If there is an antecedent in the sentence, circle it.

EXAMPLE: _____Some_____ of the (audience) hooted and clapped.

1. _____ in the music shed applauded.

2. _____ of the original manuscript was lost.

3. In *Bums*, Peter Golenbock wrote about _____ of the old Dodgers.

4. I have _____ of the ingredients for the rhubarb pie.

5. My grandmother seems to know a little about _____.

17.1 **Pronouns • Practice 2**

▶ **Exercise 1** **Recognizing Antecedents.** Write the antecedent of each underlined pronoun. If an antecedent is implied, write *implied*.

EXAMPLE: The candidate for <u>whom</u> I voted lost the election. _____candidate   implied_____

1. As the boy bicycled down the road, <u>he</u> whistled. _____
2. Ann must get <u>herself</u> ready if <u>she</u> wants to be on time. _____
3. <u>My</u> father told me to give my sister <u>her</u> lunch. _____
4. It was my sister's birthday, but the family gave <u>her</u> a present <u>that</u> was meant for me. _____
5. Jody <u>himself</u> admitted to planning the prank. _____
6. Ray thinks <u>his</u> new car looks very clean next to ours. _____
7. The three girls packed <u>themselves</u> plenty of food for <u>their</u> hike. _____
8. Those are the shoes I want, but Mother says <u>she</u> will not buy them for me. _____
9. We rode in a taxicab <u>whose</u> driver drove expertly. _____
10. Grant connected <u>his</u> stereo and then sat listening to <u>it</u>. _____

▶ **Exercise 2** **Identifying Different Types of Pronouns.** Write *personal, reflexive, intensive, demonstrative, relative, interrogative,* or *indefinite* to indicate the type of each underlined pronoun.

EXAMPLE: For nearly three hundred years, Saint Bernards have been used to rescue people <u>who</u> were buried alive in deep snow. _____relative_____

When snow (1) <u>that</u> is held in place by friction is dislodged, (2) <u>it</u> can cause a serious avalanche. (3) <u>This</u> is a vast amount of snow cascading down a mountainside. The snow (4) <u>itself</u> can exert over 22,000 pounds of pressure per square inch and travel over 192 miles per hour. (5) <u>Few</u> caught in an avalanche can save (6) <u>themselves</u>, but Saint Bernards have been trained to locate victims. They have rescued over 2,500 people during (7) <u>their</u> nearly three hundred years of service. (8) <u>Which</u> of the dogs has the best rescue record? (9) <u>None</u> of the animals has a more impressive list than Barry, (10) <u>who</u> saved over forty avalanche victims.

1. _____   6. _____
2. _____   7. _____
3. _____   8. _____
4. _____   9. _____
5. _____   10. _____

▶ **Exercise 3** **Using the Correct Pronoun.** Complete the paragraph by filling in each blank with the kind of pronoun indicated in parentheses.

EXAMPLE: The tents were clustered under the tall pines, _____which_____ (relative) rustled gently in the breeze.

The sun revealed (1) _____ (reflexive) as (2) _____ (personal) burst forth from behind the clouds (3) _____ (relative) hid it. The sun's rays soon warmed the campers, and (4) _____ (personal) awoke, rubbing the sleep from (5) _____ (personal) eyes. The children (6) _____ (intensive) were responsible for tidying up and for preparing breakfast, so the campsite was quickly bustling with activity. (7) _____ (indefinite) of the children worked very hard, and before long, the aroma of freshly made cocoa filled the air. "(8) _____ (interrogative) wants breakfast!" shouted the cooks. "(9) _____ (demonstrative) is (10) _____ (personal) last call!"

17.2 Action Verbs and Linking Verbs • Practice 1

Action Verbs and Linking Verbs An action verb tells what action someone or something is performing. A linking verb connects its subject with another word that renames or describes the subject.

Action Verbs	Linking Verbs
The fire siren *sounded*.	Adams *was* our second President.
Tiffany *smiled* at the photographer.	The moon *seems* unusually small.

▶ **Exercise 1** **Identifying Action and Linking Verbs.** Write *action* or *linking* after each underlined verb.

EXAMPLE: Whitney is *our* coach. ___*linking*___

1. The telephone <u>rings</u> in both offices. _____
2. Milk <u>turns</u> bad quickly unless refrigerated. _____
3. Grandfather <u>grew</u> cucumbers during the summer. _____
4. The injured man <u>stumbled</u> into the hospital. _____
5. Two hours late, the bus <u>pulled</u> into the station. _____
6. His forehead <u>feels</u> cool to the touch. _____
7. Brian <u>memorized</u> the opening line of his speech. _____
8. Winter <u>will arrive</u> on December 21. _____
9. After the accident, he <u>looked</u> pale and worried. _____
10. The express bus <u>may be</u> late this evening. _____

▶ **Exercise 2** **Using Linking Verbs.** From the list below, choose an appropriate linking verb to use in each of the following sentences.

appear	seem	grow	look	be
smell	taste	sound	become	feel

EXAMPLE: The stew ___*tasted*___ delicious.

1. The flowers _____ sweet and fresh.
2. In the morning Mother _____ sick.
3. He certainly _____ qualified for the position.
4. The band _____ louder than usual.
5. The actress _____ more excited than usual.
6. Margaret _____ captain of our softball team.
7. The pudding _____ sour.
8. Before each performance Sue _____ tense.
9. He _____ our chairman last year.
10. The sky _____ dark and threatening.

17.2 Action Verbs and Linking Verbs • Practice 2

▶ **Exercise 1**   **Identifying Action and Linking Verbs.**   Identify each underlined verb as an *action verb* or *linking verb*.

EXAMPLE: The puppy <u>grew</u> bigger every day. ____*linking verb*____

1. The kitten <u>raced</u> around the living room. _____
2. I <u>smelled</u> a gas leak. _____
3. Our dinner <u>should be</u> ready by now. _____
4. The accident victim <u>remained</u> unconscious. _____
5. Your behavior <u>might have been</u> less rude. _____
6. The hinges sounded rusty as I <u>pulled</u> the door open. _____
7. He <u>submitted</u> his latest poems for the contest. _____
8. The huge dog <u>was</u> ferocious. _____
9. Lisa <u>decided</u> to apply to West Point. _____
10. Our walnuts <u>tasted</u> bitter. _____
11. Frederick <u>leaned</u> back in his chair. _____
12. Theresa <u>walked</u> through the room and out onto the balcony. _____
13. The soufflé <u>was</u> light and delicious. _____
14. Camilla repeatedly <u>winked</u> at Jeremy. _____
15. The room <u>seemed</u> dark and oppressive. _____

▶ **Exercise 2**   **Writing Sentences with Verbs.**   Write a sentence that includes the kind of verb indicated in parentheses.

EXAMPLE: (linking verb) ____*This stew seems quite spicy.*____

1. (action verb) _____
2. (linking verb) _____
3. (action verb) _____
4. (linking verb) _____
5. (action verb) _____
6. (linking verb) _____
7. (action verb) _____
8. (linking verb) _____
9. (action verb) _____
10. (linking verb) _____
11. (action verb) _____
12. (linking verb) _____
13. (action verb) _____
14. (linking verb) _____
15. (action verb) _____

17.2 Transitive and Intransitive Verbs • Practice 1

Transitive and Intransitive Verbs An action verb is *transitive* if it directs action toward someone or something named in the same sentence. An action verb is *intransitive* if it does not direct action toward someone or something named in the same sentence.

Transitive	Intransitive
Marie *opened* the package.	Marie *spoke* into the mike.
The catcher *chose* a large, soft mitt.	The catcher *shouted* angrily.

> **Exercise 1** **Identifying Transitive and Intransitive Verbs.** Label each underlined verb as *transitive* or *intransitive* on the line to the right of each sentence.

EXAMPLE: The roof leaks at the first sign of rain. _____*intransitive*_____

1. Keith placed the heavy metal turntable on his desk. _____
2. Clouds swirled near the top of the mountain. _____
3. After much delay the judge rendered an unpopular decision. _____
4. Did you buy the vegetables for the stew? _____
5. East Hampton is not far from Shelter Island. _____
6. For a good analysis, read *Understanding Fiction.* _____
7. Vicki rehearsed her speech many times. _____
8. The runaway bus careened into a stone wall. _____
9. City dwellers always enjoy a trip into the country. _____
10. The orchestra began with a loud overture. _____

> **Exercise 2** **Writing Sentences with Transitive and Intransitive Verbs.** Complete the sentences below. For sentences with transitive verbs, add a noun or pronoun toward which the verb directs its actions.

EXAMPLE: Transitive: Bruce made an important ____*choice*____ .
  Intransitive: Sally smiled ____*up at us*____ .

1. Transitive: After dinner, Ted read a _____
2. Intransitive: The motorcycle races _____ .
3. Intransitive: The library opens _____ .
4. Transitive: My brother bought a _____ .
5. Transitive: I mailed the _____ yesterday.
6. Intransitive: Suddenly, the town appeared _____ .
7. Intransitive: My father laughed _____ .
8. Transitive: Take the _____ into the kitchen.
9. Transitive: We welcomed the _____ to our city.
10. Intransitive: In the morning the birds chirp _____ .

17.2 Transitive and Intransitive Verbs • Practice 2

► Exercise 1 **Identifying Transitive and Intransitive Verbs.** Underline the verbs, labeling each as *transitive* or *intransitive.*

1. The townspeople took a siesta each afternoon. _____

2. For a few extra dollars each week, she ironed clothes. _____

3. The mother smiled at the infant in her arms. _____

4. The eel slid along the floor of the ocean. _____

5. The crew ate lunch under an old oak tree. _____

6. We purchased tickets for the play *The Incredible Day.* _____

7. The pup tent collapsed from the high winds. _____

8. Our neighbors continually complain about our dog. _____

9. With reluctance, he swallowed the medicine. _____

10. Time stretched before us. _____

11. Myra served the tea to her three friends. _____

12. Opal took the flowers from Roberta. _____

13. Steven ice-skated for three hours. _____

14. The puppy trembled in the cold. _____

15. John's words would live forever in my memory. _____

► Exercise 2 **Identifying Transitive and Intransitive Verbs.** For each sentence, underscore either *transitive* or *intransitive* to indicate how each verb is used.

1. Janet walked out of the department store. (transitive, intransitive)

   Janet walked the dog for about forty-five minutes. (transitive, intransitive)

2. Stuart left the kitten with the mother cat. (transitive, intransitive)

   Stuart left for school at about eight o'clock. (transitive, intransitive)

3. The infant cried for her mother. (transitive, intransitive)

   The infant cried salty tears. (transitive, intransitive)

4. Janet woke at dawn. (transitive, intransitive)

   Janet woke her brother at dawn. (transitive, intransitive)

5. Leila photographed the lizard on the rock. (transitive, intransitive)

   Leila photographed for two hours. (transitive, intransitive)

6. The terrible expense increased the pressure on Jim. (transitive, intransitive)

   Jim's expenses increased each year. (transitive, intransitive)

7. Dan led Victoria gracefully around the dance floor. (transitive, intransitive)

   On the dance floor, Dan led confidently. (transitive, intransitive)

8. The leaves of the trees shook in the wind. (transitive, intransitive)

   The wind shook the leaves in the trees. (transitive, intransitive)

9. The cat is shedding all over the furniture. (transitive, intransitive)

   The snake is shedding its skin. (transitive, intransitive)

10. Ted and Susan visited a historical landmark this afternoon. (transitive, intransitive)

    Ted and Susan visited for three hours this afternoon. (transitive, intransitive)

17.2 Verb Phrases • Practice 1

Verb Phrases   A verb that has more than one word is a verb phrase. A verb phrase is formed by adding a helping verb to another verb in a sentence.

VERB PHRASES

The train *will arrive* at noon.
The trip *should have taken* three hours.
The battle *might have been* won more easily.
She *has* already *made* her choice.
I *will* definitely not *leave* until tomorrow.

Exercise 1   **Identifying Verb Phrases.**   Underline all parts of the verb phrase in each sentence. Do not underline the words that interrupt a verb phrase.

EXAMPLE: Unfortunately, I could not find the evidence.

1. By now, we should have been in Boston.
2. The police department has already been notified.
3. We can expect a letter from them in a month.
4. The flood has not blocked the main highway.
5. Their roles have not been clearly defined.
6. The doctor should have given you a more complete diagnosis.
7. Obviously, the trip must have taken several hours longer.
8. Will you remind them of our change in plans?
9. The senator did undoubtedly intend a postponement of the bill.
10. Can I really have forgotten their anniversary?

Exercise 2   **Using Verb Phrases.**   Fill in the blanks in each sentence with appropriate verb phrases.

EXAMPLE: She ____should____ ____be____ ____arriving____ soon.

1. _____ you _____ a birthday card for your sister?
2. I _____ always _____ my responsibilities.
3. If I wanted, I _____ _____ _____ a different route.
4. _____ you ever _____ New Hampshire?
5. I _____ not _____ about the accident.
6. Our family _____ _____ to attend the summer Olympics.
7. They _____ _____ to go much earlier.
8. My stereo _____ not highly _____ by *Consumer Reports*.
9. _____ not _____ a caustic cleaning agent.
10. If we had trained harder,
    we _____ _____ _____ them.

17.2 Verb Phrases • Practice 2

▶ **Exercise 1** **Using Verb Phrases.** Fill in the blanks with appropriate verb phrases.

EXAMPLE: We ___*have*___ ___*been*___ ___*working*___ in the yard.

1. The train _____ _____ _____ the station soon.
2. We _____ probably not _____ the wedding next week.
3. The car _____ _____ along the freeway.
4. _____ I _____ a present for my sister?
5. The vacationers _____ _____ money from their bank.
6. The fields _____ a week ago.
7. I _____ _____ in a special performance.
8. Instead of talking, I _____ definitely _____ now.
9. The house _____ _____ _____ before we move in.
10. I _____ not _____ this book.
11. The editor _____ _____ the manuscript carefully.
12. Mark _____ _____ _____ on his paper for two weeks.
13. Ida _____ not _____ the book yet.
14. The baby _____ _____ for twenty minutes.
15. Jackie _____ certainly _____ to attend the party.

▶ **Writing Application** **Writing Sentences with Different Kinds of Verbs.** Write ten sentences of your own, using the verbs given in the form indicated in parentheses.

EXAMPLE: seem (as a linking verb)
_____*The bridge seemed safe.*_____

1. look (as in an action verb)

_____

2. look (as in a linking verb)

_____

3. rest (as a transitive verb)

_____

4. rest (as an intransitive verb)

_____

5. help (with two helping verbs)

_____

6. help (as a transitive verb)

_____

7. appear (as a linking verb)

_____

8. appear (with one helping verb)

_____

9. dismiss (as an intransitive verb)

_____

10. dismiss (as a transitive verb)

_____

17.3 **Adjectives • Practice 1**

Adjectives An adjective is a word used to describe a noun or pronoun or to give a noun or pronoun a more specific meaning. Like nouns, adjectives can be compound—that is, they can be made up of more than one word—or proper. Proper adjectives are formed from proper nouns and always begin with a capital letter. A pronoun is used as an adjective if it modifies a noun. The chart below summarizes the kinds of pronouns used as adjectives and their use.

Possessive Adjectives		Demonstrative Adjectives	Interrogative Adjectives	Indefinite Adjectives			
				Singular	**Plural**	**Either**	
my	its	this	which	another	both	all	most
your	our	that	what	each	few	any	other
his	their	these	whose	either	many	more	some
her		those		neither	several		

▷ **Exercise 1** **Recognizing Compound Adjectives and Proper Adjectives.** Underline the compound or proper adjective in each sentence.

EXAMPLE: The first <u>European</u> settlement in Delaware was made by Swedes.

1. The meat-packing industry is very large in Brazil.
2. The river flows from the Canadian Rockies to the Pacific.
3. Jim gave Rita his wholehearted support.
4. It took three years to build the underground tunnel.
5. Dad served Hawaiian pineapple for desert.
6. Kim took a headlong dive into the lake.
7. We ordered French dressing on our salads.
8. The attendant served dinner on the cross-country flight.
9. This juice comes from Algerian oranges.
10. Sara saw a Shakespearean play last Friday.

▷ **Exercise 2** **Adding Pronouns Used as Adjectives.** Fill in each blank with the kind of adjective given in parentheses.

EXAMPLE: Bill hung ____*his*____ coat in the closet. (possessive)

1. _____ people are planning to visit Washington, D.C., for the Apple-Blossom Festival. (indefinite)
2. This sweater costs more than _____ one. (demonstrative)
3. _____ apples are best for baking? (interrogative)
4. _____ car is blocking the driveway? (interrogative)
5. Joan brought _____ cousin to the school picnic. (possessive)
6. Are _____ bananas ripe yet? (demonstrative)
7. Judy and Frank gave _____ report on Wednesday. (possessive)
8. _____ couples are going to Diane's house. (indefinite)
9. Do you remember where you put _____ umbrella? (possessive)
10. _____ reporter wanted the assignment. (indefinite)

17.3 **Adjectives • Practice 2**

▶ **Exercise 1** **Identifying Adjectives.** Find all the adjectives, if any, that modify each underlined noun or pronoun. Then draw an arrow from each adjective to the word it modifies.

EXAMPLE: The statue fell *there*.

(1) Insects seem as indestructible as (2) they are innumerable. Most (3) experts say that one (4) reason

for this is their (5) ability to adapt to different (6) environments. Some (7) insects can live in icebound

(8) streams while (9) others prefer hot (10) springs that may reach 50°C. Their small (11) size also accounts

for their continued (12) survival. Some North American (13) insects measure one one-hundredth of an inch,

and that size makes (14) them hard to see and even harder to exterminate. But their amazing (15) power to

reproduce probably contributes most to their (16) durability. Generally, these prolific (17) creatures can

reproduce several (18) times during one (19) season. (20) Many lay enormous (21) numbers of eggs.

(22) Few can surpass a fertile queen (23) termite, which may lay 30,000 (24) eggs in a single

twenty-four-hour (25) period.

▶ **Exercise 2** **Using Adjectives in Your Own Writing.** Write five sentences, using as many different adjectives as you can to describe the color, shape, location, and condition of one of the following nouns. Do *not* start your description with such words as "It looks like…" or "It was…"

A key	A book
A house	A car
A body of water	An animal
A person	A fire
A dessert	A plant

1. _____

_____

2. _____

_____

3. _____

_____

4. _____

_____

5. _____

_____

17.3 Adverbs • Practice 1

Adverbs   An adverb is a word that modifies a verb, an adjective, or another adverb.

Adverbs Modifying Verbs	
Where? The statue fell *there*.	**When?** Beth left *yesterday*.
In what manner? The mayor walks *slowly*.	**To what extent?** Sam has *almost* completed his report.
Adverbs Modifying Adjectives	**Adverbs Modifying Adverbs**
To what extent? She was *unusually* tired.	**To what extent?** The band plays *really* well.

> **Exercise 1**   **Recognizing Adverbs and the Words They Modify.**   Underline the adverb in each sentence. In the space provided, tell whether it modifies a *verb*, an *adjective*, or *another adverb*. Some sentences have two adverbs.

EXAMPLE: Carol reacted angrily. ____*verb*____

1. My father was extremely angry. _____
2. Sandy had really wanted to go. _____
3. He said he would leave tomorrow. _____
4. Would you believe that your suitcases are there? _____
5. She will probably try to reach the governor. _____
6. Which player skates more rapidly? _____
7. Grandmother is exceedingly well. _____
8. I can hardly solve this problem. _____
9. Alice is unusually quiet today. _____
10. The accident victim recovered rather rapidly. _____

> **Exercise 2**   **Adding Adverbs to Sentences.**   Fill in the blanks below with appropriate adverbs.

EXAMPLE: My sister always drives ____*carefully*____ .

1. Stan _____ displayed his award.
2. Our representative arrived in Chicago _____ .
3. Unfortunately, she is _____ handicapped.
4. Mother and father are feeling _____ well.
5. She has _____ disagreed with us.
6. I think he is _____ sorry.
7. They were _____ distressed by his reply.
8. Which one types _____ rapidly?
9. A shopping mall is located _____ .
10. Father _____ turned into a dead end.

17.3 Adverbs • Practice 2

> **Exercise 1**   **Identifying Adverbs.**   Underline all the adverbs. Then draw an arrow from each adverb to the word or words it modifies.

EXAMPLE: The rapidly approaching storm had been predicted.

1. The surf-casters carried their large catch of fish triumphantly.
2. During the hike, the tired little boy fell steadily behind.
3. Unexpectedly, the ball sailed toward the new picture window.
4. The instructions were completely accurate, and we arrived soon afterward.
5. Tomorrow we must leave extremely early.
6. The package had been wrapped tightly and professionally.
7. You will find the office if you go straight and turn left at the very first intersection.
8. Eventually, they will restore this historic landmark totally.
9. The boys ran quite hastily toward the wrecked car.
10. They have partially tiled the new roof and will finish it soon.

> **Exercise 2**   **Adding Adverbs.**   Fill in the blanks with appropriate adverbs.

    (1)_____ perched in the top of the Superdome, a family is
(2) _____ watching a circus (3) _____. It is
(4) _____ odd to see a high-wire act ten floors (5) _____. But that
happens at the (6) _____ large Louisiana Superdome. The Superdome can
(7) _____ astound even the (8) _____ casual observer. A tour alone
leads the visitor (9) _____ a maze of twists and turns, (10) _____
covering over two miles. This (11) _____ massive structure reaches
(12) _____ for (13) _____ twenty-seven stories; the replay monitor,
(14) _____ located, is composed of six individual screens, each one the size of a
(15) _____ large living-room floor.

> **Writing Application**   **Writing Sentences with Adjectives and Adverbs.**   If the underlined word is an adjective, write a sentence using it as an adverb. If the underlined word is an adverb, use it in a sentence as an adjective. You may change endings of the underlined words.

EXAMPLE: She handed me only one dollar.   *Beth is an only child.*

1. The deep lake held some huge bass.

   _____

2. Frank talked loudly so that we could hear him.

   _____

3. The rocket shot high into the air.

   _____

4. That razor does not give me a close shave.

   _____

5. Draw a straight line connecting points A and B.

   _____

17.4 Prepositions • Practice 1

Prepositions   A preposition is a word that relates a noun or pronoun following it to another word in the sentence.

FREQUENTLY USED PREPOSITIONS				
above	before	for	near	through
across	below	from	of	to
among	between	in	on	under

A prepositional phrase begins with a preposition and ends with a noun or pronoun called the object of the preposition.

PREPOSITIONAL PHRASES	
Prepositions	**Objects of Prepositions**
at	the station
near	them
in	a long dark corridor

▶ **Exercise 1**   **Identifying Prepositions.**   Underline each preposition in the sentences below. Some sentences have more than one.

EXAMPLE: Tommy crawled <u>between</u> the fence and the wall.

1. Fortunately, we left the motel at dawn.

2. Among his friends he numbers several prominent doctors.

3. She was deeply respected for her honesty.

4. The man with the briefcase is an undercover agent.

5. In certain instances we must simply hope for the best.

6. We found the map under a pile of library books.

7. Before daylight, the troops filed across the bridge.

8. About an hour later, they marched into a large town.

9. My sister received a letter from a chance acquaintance.

10. To me, there is no comparison between the two singers.

▶ **Exercise 2**   **Identifying Prepositional Phrases.**   In each sentence place parentheses around each prepositional phrase. Some sentences have more than one.

EXAMPLE: She waited (for us) (in the restaurant).

1. He won three medals by the end of the tournament.

2. The speaker near the podium is the senator from Texas.

3. At the station she ran into her old boyfriend.

4. The treasure was buried under the red barn.

5. We learned about computers in our math class.

6. The girl with us at the party lives in Ohio.

7. Several rockets shot directly across the battlefield.

8. He was identified by a mole on his right shoulder.

9. A thunderous sound echoed through the corridor.

10. On balance, she is the best gymnast of the competition.

17.4 Prepositions • Practice 2

▶ **Exercise 1** **Identifying Prepositional Phrases.** Place parentheses around the prepositional phrase or prepositional phrases in each sentence. Then underline each preposition and circle each object.

EXAMPLE: Sit (beside (me)) and tell me (about your (trip)).

1. In back of the shop the owner and his son baked fresh bread every day.
2. Step outside the door and see the sunset.
3. We ran out of money during our shopping expedition.
4. According to the President's speech, we need a greater awareness of pollution problems.
5. Chinese lanterns were hung from the ceiling.
6. David carefully placed the delicate glass figurine next to the vase.
7. The terrified rabbit slipped between the fence posts and ran to safety.
8. Billy the Kid stayed ahead of his pursuers by means of a stolen horse.
9. Don't walk in the storm without a hat and boots.
10. The exhausted long-distance runner finally fell behind the others.

▶ **Exercise 2** **Distinguishing Between Prepositions and Adverbs.** Identify each underlined word as either a *preposition* or an *adverb*. If the word is a preposition, write its object.

EXAMPLE: Above, the sun shone brightly. _____adverb_____

1. You will have the shovel outside the door of the shed.
2. The captain sent the passengers below during the storm.
3. I saw that movie over and over.
4. The painter climbed up the ladder.
5. The paper airplane sailed around and then crashed.
6. At noon, the doctor went out.
7. Because of the rain the practice was held inside today.
8. The speed skater raced around the turn.
9. The flower pot fell off the sill.
10. The smoke drifted lazily up the chimney.

▶ **Exercise 3** **Using Prepositional Phrases.** Fill in the blanks with appropriate prepositional phrases.

EXAMPLE: I was almost late _____for the track meet_____ yesterday.

The track meet was scheduled (1) _____, and we were told to meet

(2) _____. As usual, I was "running" late. (Did you catch that pun?) I found my

running shoes (3) _____; my track shorts were (4) _____.

Finally, I dashed (5) _____ but the bus had already left

(6) _____. I raced home and asked my mother (7) _____. She

agreed and I got (8) _____. My mother is a cautious driver, and we crawled along

(9) _____. When I arrived, I had five minutes to prepare

(10) _____.

17.4 Conjunctions • Practice 1

Conjunctions   A conjunction is used to connect other words or groups of words. Coordinating conjunctions and correlative conjunctions join similar kinds of words or groups of words that are grammatically alike.

COORDINATING CONJUNCTIONS
and   but   for   nor   or   so   yet

CORRELATIVE CONJUNCTIONS
both . . . and   either . . . or   neither . . . nor whether . . . or   not only . . . but also

Subordinating conjunctions connect subordinate clauses with independent clauses in complex sentences.

FREQUENTLY USED SUBORDINATING CONJUNCTIONS				
after	as soon as	even though	than	when
although	as though	if	though	whenever
as	because	since	unless	wherever
as if	before	so that	until	while

▶ **Exercise 1**   **Identifying Conjunctions.**   Underline the conjunction in each sentence. Then write whether it is *coordinating, correlative,* or *subordinating* on the line to the right of the sentence.

EXAMPLE: As soon as she phoned, we left. ____*subordinating*____

1. I offered my help, but she refused. _____

2. Both a dictionary and a thesaurus are useful in college. _____

3. My brother has held several jobs since he graduated. _____

4. Either I will go, or I will send a representative. _____

5. When she arrived, the crowd cheered wildly. _____

6. My brother and two sisters all play sports. _____

7. He is not only neat, but he is also accurate. _____

8. I travel because I enjoy meeting new people. _____

9. Unfortunately, she knows neither French nor German. _____

10. We had a winning record while he was our captain. _____

▶ **Exercise 2**   **Using Subordinating Conjunctions in Complex Sentences.**   Complete each complex sentence below. Note the use of a comma when the subordinate clause comes first.

EXAMPLE: Unless ____*I hear from you soon*____ , I will leave early.

1. Although _____ , I was unable to handle it.

2. You must read all your notes if _____ .

3. When _____ , Mom will lend you her car.

4. Bill goes to the gym whenever _____ .

5. As _____ , Brenda was in the wrong.

Name _____ Date _____

17.4 Conjunctions • Practice 2

▶ **Exercise 1** **Identifying Conjunctions in Sentences.** Underline the conjunctions. Then identify each as *coordinating*, *correlative*, or *subordinating*.

EXAMPLE: I looked for Liz, but I could not find her. _____coordinating_____

1. Either we leave now or we don't go at all. _____
2. I want Rosa and you to play the leads in the play. _____
3. Before we have lunch, I want to swim some laps. _____
4. I will bake a cake so that we have enough for the sale. _____
5. We will stay until they hand out the awards. _____
6. White, blue, or beige upholstery would suit this room. _____
7. Even though he has little experience, I plan to hire him for the job. _____
8. Will you get the phone, for I have to leave right now. _____
9. Since we weeded the garden, the whole yard looks better. _____
10. It doesn't matter to me if you take Brian to the park. _____

▶ **Exercise 2** **Distinguishing Between Subordinating Conjunctions, Prepositions, and Adverbs.** Identify each underlined word as a *subordinating conjunction*, *preposition*, or *adverb*.

EXAMPLE: It has been a year since they moved away. _____subordinating conjunction_____

1. They have been out fishing since dawn. _____
2. When does school begin? _____
3. You will have to wait until the test is given again. _____
4. The results will not be published till June. _____
5. I will meet you where we met last week. _____
6. My knees began to shake when they called my name. _____
7. We had visited Mexico once before. _____
8. After the fifteenth, we can pick up our checks. _____
9. Where are the suitcases kept? _____
10. I had no idea that job-hunting could be so tiring until today. _____

▶ **Exercise 3** **Using Conjunctive Adverbs.** Rewrite each pair of sentences, inserting an appropriate conjunctive adverb to connect the related ideas.

EXAMPLE: The ship's engine broke down. The Coast Guard had to tow it to port.
   The ship's engine broke down; consequently, the Coast Guard had to tow it to port.

1. I must turn the report in on time. My grade will be lowered.

_____

2. He wanted to buy a condominium. He looked at several.

_____

3. I do not want to cook. We have no food in the house.

_____

4. She missed the ship. She had to fly to the next port to meet it.

_____

5. I work at a department store. I write feature articles in my spare time.

_____

© Prentice-Hall, Inc.

17.4 Interjections • Practice 1

Interjections   An interjection is a word that expresses strong feeling or emotion and has no grammatical connection to the sentence in which it appears.

SOME COMMON INTERJECTIONS				
ah	dear	hey	ouch	well
aha	goodness	hurray	psst	whew
alas	gracious	oh	tsk	wow

Interjections are set off from the rest of the sentence by either a comma or an exclamation mark.

▶ Exercise 1   Identifying Interjections.   Underline the interjection in each sentence below.

EXAMPLE: <u>Well</u>, I guess we lost again.

1. Oh! I cannot find my keys, and I don't have a spare set.
2. Psst, is this the way to the stadium?
3. Hurray! We finally reached the playoffs.
4. Grandmother said, "Gracious, why is Uncle Burt always late?"
5. Alas, the princess rejected her suitor once again.
6. One of grandpa's favorite expressions was "tsk!"
7. Whew! I am glad we reached the station on time.
8. "Ouch, that hurts," I told my dentist.
9. My aunt said, "Goodness, that music is loud."
10. "Hey, wait for me," Vic said as he caught his breath.

▶ Exercise 2   Writing Sentences with Interjections.   Write an appropriate sentence using each interjection below.

EXAMPLE: Hurray! _____I passed my final examination_____ .

1. Oh, _____ .
2. Aunt Sally whispered, "Goodness, _____ ."
3. Aha! _____ .
4. Jim began, "Well, _____ ."
5. Mother exclaimed, "Whew, _____ !"
6. Hurray! _____ .
7. The knight sighed, "Alas, _____ ."
8. Psst! Tell me, _____ ?
9. The manager cried, "Wow, _____ ."
10. Ouch, _____ .

17.4 Interjections • Practice 2

▶ **Exercise 1** **Using Interjections.** Write ten sentences using an appropriate interjection to express the emotion or feeling indicated. Then, underline each interjection.

EXAMPLE: regret   *Oh, I wish you could go with us.*

1. joy _____
2. pain _____
3. hesitation _____
4. surprise _____
5. impatience _____
6. anger _____
7. sorrow _____
8. disappointment _____
9. disgust _____
10. excitement _____

▶ **Writing Application** **Using Prepositions, Conjunctions, and Interjections to Expand Sentences.** Expand each sentence by adding at least one preposition, one conjunction, or one interjection, as well as any other words that are necessary. Write the new sentences, circling the prepositions, underlining the conjunctions once, and underlining the interjections twice.

EXAMPLE: I prepared the dessert.
    Jody and I prepared the dessert (for) dinner.

1. I played my new CD.

   _____

2. The campfire blazed.

   _____

3. The noise awoke the entire neighborhood.

   _____

4. Twenty gray pigeons landed suddenly.

   _____

5. The artist used green paint.

   _____

6. Your cat seems to be fighting.

   _____

7. Have you heard that athletic shoes are on sale?

   _____

8. Jeannie, come to my house at four.

   _____

9. I didn't know you were waiting.

   _____

10. Did you see the elephants?

   _____

17.5 Words as Different Parts of Speech
• Practice 1

Identifying Parts of Speech The way a word is used in a sentence determines what part of speech it is.

DIFFERENT USES OF A WORD
As a noun: I purchased a FM *radio*.
As a verb: In an emergency, *radio* for help.
As an adjective: I will use a *radio* transmission.

▶ **Exercise 1** **Identifying Parts of Speech.** On each blank at the right, write the part of speech of each underlined word.

EXAMPLE: Ted had a good <u>run</u> this morning. _____*noun*_____
<u>Run</u> into the house for the charcoal. _____*verb*_____

1. The audience <u>rose</u> when the judge entered. _____
2. She put a single <u>rose</u> in the vase. _____
3. Who can forget King's "I Have a <u>Dream</u>" speech? _____
4. There is a <u>dream</u> sequence in the film. _____
5. <u>After</u> school, I have a part-time job. _____
6. <u>After</u> she sang, she left the stage immediately. _____
7. We decided to take the <u>slow</u>, scenic route. _____
8. <u>Slow</u> the engine gradually. _____
9. <u>Ice</u> the vegetables for a few minutes before serving. _____
10. Use some <u>ice</u> to reduce the inflammation. _____

▶ **Exercise 2** **Finding Parallel Parts of Speech.** The chart below contains columns for nouns, verbs, adjectives, and adverbs. Place each given word in as many other columns as you can.

	NOUN	VERB	ADJECTIVE	ADVERB
EXAMPLE:		clean	*clean*	
1.	hunger	_____	_____	_____
2.	_____	care	_____	_____
3.	_____	_____	early	_____
4.	_____	_____	_____	left
5.	river	_____	_____	_____

Words as Different Parts of Speech
• Practice 2

▷ **Exercise 1**   **Identifying Parts of Speech.**   Write the part of speech of the two underlined words in each sentence.

EXAMPLE: Put the ice away and then ice the cake. _____*noun, verb*_____

1. The garden hose should be near the rose garden. _____
2. We run the dogs once each day in the dog run out back. _____
3. I don't like either, but I must pick either one or the other. _____
4. I will not iron with this iron. _____
5. The chair fell over and then rolled over the rug. _____
6. Gracious, they were very gracious hosts at the party. _____
7. I hope my good grade will increase your hope of getting one. _____
8. Please turn the light on and put the groceries on the table. _____
9. She rubbed hard on the hard surface of the table to restore its shine. _____
10. The children comb their hair with the blue comb on the dresser. _____

▷ **Exercise 2**   **More Work with Parts of Speech.**   Write the part of speech of each underlined word.

EXAMPLE: When and where did fans first originate? _____*adverb*_____

(1) From _____ (2) historians _____ we learn that the

Chinese used fans as early as 3000 B.C. It (3) is _____ also known that

(4) the _____ rulers of Egypt were (5) efficiently _____ cooled by

(6) palm _____ fans. Serving an important (7) function _____ in

early (8) religious _____ ceremonies, fans (9) brushed _____

flies (10) away _____ from sacred vessels. By 700 A.D., the

(11) Japanese _____ invented (12) folding _____ fans

(13) and _____ added bright colors to (14) them _____ ;

(15) however _____ , it is the Portuguese (16) whom _____ we

can thank for introducing fans to Europe (17) in _____ the 1500's. So popular were

(18) they _____ that (19) many _____ of the men

(20) during _____ the reign of Louis XV carried them. Artists of the 1800's painted

fans, and the (21) works _____ of great masters grace the folds of some fans.

(22) Alas _____ , fans are used (23) today _____ primarily as

(24) wallhangings _____ , seldom as part (25) of _____ our attire.

18.1 Complete Subjects and Predicates
• Practice 1

Complete Subjects and Predicates   A sentence is a group of words with two main parts: a complete subject and a complete predicate. Together these parts express a complete thought.

Complete Subjects	Complete Predicates
The elegant schooner	still sails majestically.
A girl wearing a yellow scarf	will meet you at the ferry.
Wheat germ	is nutritious.

▶ **Exercise 1**   **Recognizing Complete Subjects and Predicates.**   Draw a vertical line between each complete subject and predicate.

EXAMPLE: The roof of the barn | collapsed suddenly.

1. Ellen and her friends visited the Modern Museum of Art.
2. You will need a good college dictionary and some other reference texts.
3. Rounding the bend, we saw the old village store under an immense elm tree.
4. Everyone must pass the same entrance examinations.
5. The end of the play was not at all surprising.
6. The road leading to the top of the peak was closed.
7. The batter lofted a long fly to the center field wall.
8. We explored the Evangeline Trail in Nova Scotia.
9. Piles of leaves and an ancient rake sat in the front yard.
10. Gore Vidal has written several good historical novels.

▶ **Exercise 2**   **Writing Complete Subjects and Predicates.**   Each item below offers either a complete subject or a complete predicate. Supply the rest of the sentence.

EXAMPLE: The people next door _____.

The people next door ___*enjoy walking in the country*___.

1. The guests in the hotel _____.
2. _____ visit each other during the summer.
3. The nearest shopping mall _____.
4. _____ eat much too rapidly.
5. My favorite movie star _____.
6. _____ was lost some time ago.
7. The keys to the car _____.
8. _____ is my favorite dessert.
9. His most frequent excuse _____.
10. _____ cannot really be explained.

18.1 Complete Subjects and Predicates
• Practice 2

▶ **Exercise 1** **Recognizing Complete Subjects and Predicates.** Underline each complete subject and circle each complete predicate.

EXAMPLE: The tall stranger (tipped his hat politely) .

1. My grandmother knitted a sweater.
2. The ruler was only eight inches long.
3. The parachuters jumped from the plane.
4. Tomorrow I will clean out the cupboard.
5. Snails and aphids ruined my garden.
6. Lilting melodies filled the air around us.
7. I ate chocolate cookies, roast beef, and iced pineapple at the fair.
8. Yesterday her rash had almost disappeared.
9. The class dissected and studied the specimens.
10. A new brand of cereal came out on the market recently.
11. The couple at the head table came all the way from Rochester.
12. The jury has been deliberating for over fourteen hours.
13. Peanut butter and grape jelly is my favorite sandwich filling.
14. Computers and the Internet have revolutionized modern communications.
15. Fifteen miles seems much too far to walk in one day.
16. *Of Mice and Men* is the title of a book by John Steinbeck.
17. Physics is the study of light, heat, sound, mechanics, and electricity.
18. Either my sister or my brother is going to help you.
19. The planning committee cannot decide on a theme for the dance.
20. Neither the doctor nor the nurse is willing to take responsibility for the error.

▶ **Exercise 2** **Writing Sentences.** Write a sentence that includes each subject or verb given below. Then in each sentence, underline the complete subject once and the complete predicate twice.

EXAMPLE: skills: *Good communication skills can help a person succeed.*

1. uncle: _____
2. Marsha and Frankie: _____
3. chimpanzees and gorillas: _____
4. baseball: _____
5. carrots, onions, and celery: _____
6. provide: _____
7. study: _____
8. performed: _____
9. practiced: _____
10. hoped: _____

Sentence or Fragment? • Practice 1

Sentence or Fragment?   A fragment is a group of words that does not express a complete thought.

Fragments	Complete Sentences
The room in the attic.	The room in the attic remained closed for many years.
Welcomed the visitors.	My grandparents and I welcomed the visitors.
On a cool, damp morning.	On a cool, damp morning, I left to join the navy.

The first fragment contains a complete subject; it needs a predicate. The second fragment contains a complete predicate; it needs a complete subject. The third fragment is a phrase; it needs both a complete subject and a complete predicate.

▷ **Exercise 1**   **Distinguishing Between Sentences and Fragments.**   In the blanks below, write *S* for each sentence and *F* for each fragment.

EXAMPLE: The bus screeched to a stop. _____S_____

1. Choose to lead the team. _____
2. Suddenly, at the crack of dawn. _____
3. The house is fenced in on three sides. _____
4. The assistant principal of the high school. _____
5. Near the top of the second mountain range. _____
6. Fish spoils rapidly unless refrigerated. _____
7. The next play written by Tennessee Williams. _____
8. Really cannot be explained without further investigation. _____
9. Gloria Eriksen is a graphic artist. _____
10. The second restaurant in the guide. _____

▷ **Exercise 2**   **Changing Fragments into Sentences.**   Decide what is missing and change the fragments into complete sentences.

EXAMPLE: on the second day   _On the second day, we reached the coast._

1. told his story _____
2. the boy in the hall _____
3. at breakfast _____
4. another slice of toast _____
5. with their help _____
6. finished her report _____
7. near the stream _____
8. the locomotive _____
9. sank to the bottom _____
10. their first attempt _____

18.1 Sentence or Fragment? • Practice 2

▶ **Exercise 1** **Locating and Correcting Sentence Fragments.** Decide whether each item is a sentence or a fragment. If it is a sentence, write *sentence*. If it is a fragment, rewrite it to make it a sentence.

EXAMPLE: After choir practice. ____*I will meet you after choir practice.*____

1. Sang a traditional melody. _____
2. A fierce wind tore at the trees. _____
3. Around the next bend. _____
4. A persistent burglar alarm. _____
5. Dodged the speeding ball. _____
6. Inhaled the fragrance of the abundant wild flowers. _____
7. An invasion from outer space was the movie's theme. _____
8. A safe speed down the hill and around the sharp turn. _____
9. Conscientious drivers always buckle their seat belts. _____
10. Handcuffed the suspect in an armed robbery. _____
11. Without a thought for his own safety. _____
12. That boy has been playing in the park for hours. _____
13. Raised her hand eagerly. _____
14. Listen to me. _____
15. A frighteningly loud and sudden noise. _____

▶ **Exercise 2** **Correcting Sentence Fragments.** The following paragraphs contain ten fragments. Underline each fragment and then, on the line below, rewrite it to make it a sentence.

Justine sat primly. On the sofa. Her hands were folded neatly. In her lap. "Is everything all right?" she asked. "Did the meeting go well?"

Stanley looked down at his shoes. Looked to the right. After that, looked up at the ceiling. Seemed to be looking everywhere but at Justine. Justine began to get nervous. "What's wrong, Stanley?" she asked.

Finally was able to find his voice. "The meeting was a disaster," he said. "The whole committee was there. Humiliated in front of everyone. All because of one error in math."

"Well, what kind of an error was it?" asked Justine.

"Just one decimal point. I thought it would cost $10,500. Instead, it was $105,000."

Justine was very disappointed. Had always been rather careless about math.

1. _____
2. _____
3. _____
4. _____
5. _____
6. _____
7. _____
8. _____
9. _____
10. _____

18.1 Simple Subjects and Predicates • Practice 1

Simple Subjects and Predicates   The simple subject is the essential noun, pronoun, or group of words acting as a noun that cannot be left out of the complete subject. The simple predicate is the essential verb or verb phrase that cannot be left out of the complete predicate. In the chart below each simple subject is underlined once, each simple predicate twice.

SIMPLE SUBJECTS AND SIMPLE PREDICATES	
Complete Subjects	**Complete Predicates**
A sudden developing storm	threatened the coastline.
The state of Alaska	has attracted settlers from many other states.

▶ **Exercise 1**   **Recognize Simple Subjects and Predicates.**   Underline the simple subject once and the simple predicate twice in the following sentences.

EXAMPLE: The old trail leads to the river bank.

1. Late one night my uncle embarked on his great adventure.
2. Beethoven completed his Pastoral Symphony in 1808.
3. The price of strawberries is unfortunately much too high.
4. The tiny island of Mauritius was granted independence by Great Britain in 1968.
5. In this part of the country rain hardly ever falls.
6. Forty-one stories by Eudora Welty were recently published.
7. Evelyn tried to reach her parents by phone.
8. A tall man in a dark raincoat waited under the streetlamp.
9. Too many excuses have been offered by the committee.
10. A killer fog resulted in 4,000 deaths in London in 1952.

▶ **Exercise 2**   **Using Simple Subjects and Predicates to Write Sentences.**   Use each simple subject and simple predicate below to write a complete sentence. Draw a vertical line between the complete subject and complete predicate.

EXAMPLE: girl won ____*A girl in my class | won an achievement award.*____

1. pilot flew _____
2. car screeched _____
3. light flickered _____
4. friend whispered _____
5. mother phoned _____
6. computer is _____
7. article discussed _____
8. brakes jammed _____
9. teacher announced _____
10. river flows _____

18.1 Simple Subjects and Predicates • Practice 2

▶**Exercise 1** **Identifying Subjects and Verbs.** In each sentence, draw a vertical line between the complete subject and the complete predicate. Then underline each subject once and each verb twice.

EXAMPLE: The geraniums | bloomed by the door.

1. Our good friends breed turkeys on their ranch.
2. The heat left us tired and uncomfortable.
3. The majority of the students voted in favor of a class trip.
4. I contemplated the words of Thoreau.
5. Many people with red hair have freckles.
6. The curtain did not rise at the scheduled time.
7. The helicopter's blades whipped the air around us.
8. I will arrange a dental appointment tomorrow.
9. My new car should arrive this week.
10. The clerks in the shoe department worked overtime today.

▶**Exercise 2** **Locating Compound Subjects and Verbs.** In each of the following sentences, underline any compound subject once and any compound verb twice.

EXAMPLE: The birds ate the crumbs and then flew away.

1. Either Clint or Helen will win the chess tournament.
2. In that race, the competitors first run and then swim.
3. The cream and sugar sat on the kitchen table within reach.
4. I added water, mixed the batter, and poured it into the pan.
5. The flora and fauna of the Amazon forest have not yet been fully cataloged and studied by scientists.
6. She received the nomination, campaigned hard, and won.
7. Carpenters, plumbers, and electricians worked here today.
8. I arrived early, waited hours, and finally got a ticket.
9. After school we held a meeting and elected Mike captain.
10. This afternoon Barbara and I baked cookies and then ate every single one of them.

▶**Writing Application** **Using Subjects and Verbs to Write Sentences.** Combine the five simple and compound subjects and the five simple and compound verbs in the following items to make five logical sentences.

airplane	battered
committee	discussed voted
wind rain	banked descended
onions garlic	were displayed were sold
stamps coins	were chopped were added

1. _____
2. _____
3. _____
4. _____
5. _____

Subjects in Different Kinds of Sentences
• Practice 1

Hard-to-Find Subjects   In most sentences the subject comes before the verb. This is called normal word order. In some sentences, however, the verb comes first, and the word order is inverted. If there is a problem finding the subject, change the sentence back to normal word order, placing the subject first.

HARD-TO-FIND SUBJECTS	
Problem Sentences	**In Normal Word Order**
On the hill is a *barn*.	A *barn* is on the hill.
There is *someone* in the house.	*Someone* is in the house.
Here is your *notebook*.	Your *notebook* is here.
Where have *you* been?	*You* have been where?
Hang up the phone.	*(You)* hang up the phone.

▶ **Exercise 1**   **Finding Hard-to-Find Subjects.**   Draw a single line under the subject and a double line under the verb.

EXAMPLE: Where did Ted put his tools?

1. There are three strange men in your office.

2. Have the grandparents arrived yet?

3. Near the bank of the river was an old canoe.

4. Where can my notebook be?

5. Here are the books from the library.

6. In the darkness lurked an incredible monster.

7. There were no right answers on the paper.

8. Will the inspector ask additional questions?

9. Through this room is an impressive library.

10. There goes the first of the marathon runners.

▶ **Exercise 2**   **Changing Sentences to Normal Word Order.**   Each sentence below is in inverted word order. Rewrite the sentence, changing it to a normal word order. Place a single line under the subject and a double line under the verb.

EXAMPLE: Under the mat is the key.

   The key is under the mat.

1. Have they opened their presents? _____

2. At the end of the road is a farmhouse. _____

3. There is a bag of flour on the shelf. _____

4. Will the train leave without us? _____

5. Here is the medical dictionary. _____

6. Down the hill skied the racer. _____

7. What have you seen? _____

8. Here is my sister. _____

9. Onto the train he walked. _____

10. Out of the country she flew. _____

18.2 Subjects in Different Kinds of Sentences
• Practice 2

Hard-to-Find Subjects

▶ **Exercise 1**   **Locating Hard-to-Find Subjects.**   In each sentence, underline the subject once and the verb twice. Write any understood words in parentheses.

EXAMPLE: Where is the meeting?

1. Finish your chores first. _____
2. Where did the customer go? _____
3. Off to the left sat the expectant hunter. _____
4. Here is the screwdriver from the tool chest. _____
5. Avalanche! _____
6. Call the store before closing time. _____
7. At what time do the gates close? _____
8. Hooray, the last day of school! _____
9. Bring the dictionaries to this room. _____
10. There sits a grand old gentleman. _____

▶ **Writing Application**   **Writing Different Kinds of Sentences with Hard-to-Find Subjects.** Use the following instructions to write ten sentences of your own.

1. Write a declarative sentence beginning with *here*.

   _____

2. Write a declarative sentence beginning with *there*.

   _____

3. Write a declarative sentence that has its subject at the end of the sentence.

   _____

4. Write an interrogative sentence beginning with a verb.

   _____

5. Write an interrogative sentence beginning with *will*.

   _____

6. Write an interrogative sentence beginning with *what*.

   _____

7. Write an imperative sentence that has an understood *you* as its subject.

   _____

8. Write an imperative sentence naming the person that is being addressed.

   _____

9. Write an exclamatory sentence beginning with *what*.

   _____

10. Write an exclamatory sentence with an understood subject and verb.

   _____

Name _____ Date _____

18.3 Direct Objects • Practice 1

Direct Objects   A complement is a word or group of words that completes the meaning of the predicate of a sentence. A direct object is a noun, pronoun, or group of words acting as a noun that receives the action of a transitive verb.

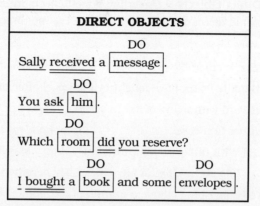

▶ **Exercise 1**   **Identifying Direct Objects.**   Draw a box around each direct object in the sentences below.

EXAMPLE: I have my own lunch .

1. My mother asked her for the cookie recipe.

2. We will need a dictionary and some paper.

3. Which television did you finally buy?

4. My uncle opened a small business in Buffalo.

5. What book do you recommend?

6. Give your notes to your homeroom teacher.

7. I told Father about your interesting offer.

8. Did Pam buy a new glass case for her glasses?

9. For the stew we need carrots, potatoes, and peas.

10. I invited him and her to the inauguration.

▶ **Exercise 2**   **Supplying Direct Objects.**   Add the necessary direct objects to the sentences below.

EXAMPLE: She gave ____them____ willingly.

1. Which _____ did you purchase?

2. For school, I will need a _____, _____, and _____.

3. Tell _____ about your experience.

4. My aunt called _____ late in the evening.

5. I want a new _____.

6. We invited _____ and _____.

7. What _____ do you like best?

8. I usually take _____ with my coffee.

9. I asked _____ about the football schedule.

10. She said you need a _____.

18.3 Direct Objects • Practice 2

Direct Objects

▶ **Exercise 1** **Recognizing Direct Objects.**   Underline direct objects in the following paragraph, including all parts of any compound direct objects. If a sentence has no direct object, write *none*.

EXAMPLE: Do you read mystery <u>stories</u>?

(1) Many mystery authors develop memorable and lasting characters in their books. _____

(2) For instance, Ellery Queen and Hercule Poirot have fought evil in novel after novel. _____

(3) Sherlock Holmes helped Scotland Yard with many of its unsolved crimes. _____ (4) In 1930, Agatha Christie's Miss Marple solved her first case. _____ (5) Readers love Perry Mason and Lieutenant Tragg. _____ (6) With unbelievable consistency, Perry Mason uncovered the vital clues in every case. _____ (7) Dorothy Gilman introduced her heroine to readers only a few years ago. _____ (8) In Gilman's book, Mrs. Pollifax, a grandmother, applies for a job as a spy with the CIA. _____ (9) Almost every young person has read the Nancy Drew and Hardy Boys mysteries. _____ (10) Recently, the movie *Murder by Death* lampooned many of the most beloved fictional detectives. _____

▶ **Exercise 2** **Writing Sentences with Direct Objects.**   Write ten sentences using the direct objects given. Write the kind of sentence indicated in parentheses.

EXAMPLE: marigolds and zinnias (question)

_____*Did you see the marigolds and zinnias?*_____

1. adventure (statement)

_____

2. broccoli and cauliflower (statement)

_____

3. triangles and squares (question)

_____

4. dachshunds and chihuahuas (statement)

_____

5. fawn (question)

_____

6. Independence Day and Thanksgiving (statement)

_____

7. kayak (question)

_____

8. morning glories, daffodils, and irises (statement)

_____

9. panther (question)

_____

10. note paper and thank-you cards (statement)

_____

18.3 Indirect Objects • Practice 1

Indirect Objects An indirect object is a noun or pronoun that appears with a direct object and names the person or thing that something is given to or done for. Note that indirect objects are found only in sentences that also have direct objects.

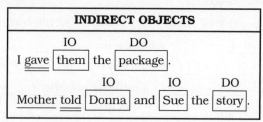

INDIRECT OBJECTS
IO   DO
I gave them the package .
IO   IO   DO
Mother told Donna and Sue the story .

Indirect objects often appear with these transitive verbs: *ask, bring, buy, give, lend, make, promise, show, teach, tell,* or *write.*

▶ **Exercise 1** **Finding Indirect Objects.** Draw a box around each indirect object in the sentences below. Underline the direct object.

EXAMPLE: She made the [baby] a new <u>sweater</u>.

1. I promised Marie and Betty tickets to the concert.

2. Show them your injury.

3. Why did you lend her your new sweater?

4. Teach the chorus the song.

5. After dinner, I gave the girls their presents.

6. Why don't you tell them the news?

7. I bought Bob and David identical gifts.

8. Mother made the boys tuna fish sandwiches.

9. I will write my old college friend a letter.

10. Bring me the plans for the new building.

▶ **Exercise 2** **Supplying Indirect Objects.** Add the necessary indirect objects to the sentences below.

EXAMPLE: I bought _____*Francie*_____ a new telephone.

1. Please lend _____ your camera.

2. Did you promise _____ another chance?

3. Later, Mrs. Wiggins told _____ the reason for her decision.

4. I will show _____ my coin collection.

5. Now give _____ your ideas about the speech.

6. I think that he will lend _____ the money.

7. I can teach _____ the procedure.

8. Tell _____ and _____ the story.

9. Nancy will buy _____ another watch.

10. We wrote _____ a strong letter.

18.3 Indirect Objects • Practice 2

▶ **Exercise 1**   **Recognizing Indirect Objects.**   Identify each underlined item as a *direct object*, *indirect object*, or *object of the preposition*.

EXAMPLE: Frank gave his friends _____*indirect object*_____ vegetables _____*direct object*_____ from his garden.

1. The employee told her boss _____ a blatant lie. _____
2. We sang the book's praises _____ to our friends. _____
3. When will Lloyd buy his sister _____ a birthday present? _____
4. The courier delivered the package _____ to him. _____
5. They drove over the hills _____ and into the village. _____
6. Terry taught herself _____ Spanish. _____
7. We wrote Aunt Emma _____ and Uncle Alvin _____ a letter.
8. I ordered soup _____ and salad _____ with my dinner.
9. Show the department store clerk _____ that faded shirt. _____
10. We cataloged the books _____ for the library. _____
11. The young father gave the new baby _____ a kiss _____ on her cheek _____.
12. Antonio tossed the ball _____ to Vincent _____.
13. Daniel sent Kurt ____ a short e-mail message _____ on Monday _____.
14. Cheryl took two crumbled sheets _____ of paper _____ out of her purse _____.
15. Henry read his little brother _____ a delightful story _____ after dinner _____.

▶ **Exercise 2**   **Writing Sentences with Objects.**   Write fifteen sentences of your own, using the direct objects (DO) and indirect objects (IO) given in parentheses.

EXAMPLE: (keys, DO; Bill, IO) _____*Melissa gave Bill the keys to the car.*_____

1. (examination, DO; patient, IO) _____
2. (slippers, DO; mother, IO) _____
3. (sweater, DO; Donald, IO) _____
4. (birthday card, DO; Cynthia, IO) _____
5. (hat, DO; Bob, IO) _____
6. (message, DO; Tina, IO) _____
7. (flowers, DO; family, IO) _____
8. (verdict, DO; judge, IO) _____
9. (cup, DO; customer, IO) _____
10. (feast, DO; guests, IO) _____
11. (collection, DO; Hector, IO) _____
12. (ladybug, DO; Jamie, IO) _____
13. (noisemakers, DO; children, IO) _____
14. (bread crumbs, DO; ducks, IO) _____
15. (parkas, DO; explorers, IO) _____

18.3 Objective Complements • Practice 1

Objective Complements An objective complement is an adjective, noun, or group of words acting as a noun that follows a direct object and describes or renames it.

OBJECTIVE COMPLEMENTS
DO OC
We <u>consider</u> Judy eligible.
DO OC
They <u>elected</u> Jason president.

Objective complements are usually found after such verbs as *appoint*, *call*, *consider*, *elect*, *label*, *make*, *name*, and *think*.

▶ **Exercise 1** **Recognizing Objective Complements.** Underline each objective complement in the sentences below. Then write whether it is a noun or an adjective.

EXAMPLE: The team chose Jeff <u>leader</u>. ___*noun*___

1. The principal appointed Steve our representative. _____

2. We painted the poster green. _____

3. Carefully label the box fragile. _____

4. Do you also consider the painting unusual? _____

5. My father often calls my brother stubborn. _____

6. Surprisingly, I found the second volume dull. _____

7. The judge ruled the decision void. _____

8. Do you think them unreasonable? _____

9. We will make Charles the treasurer. _____

10. The Student Council after much consideration named David president. _____

▶ **Exercise 2** **Writing Sentences with Objective Complements.** Add an objective complement to each sentence below. Use the part of speech given in parentheses.

EXAMPLE: We consider them ___*childish*___. (adjective)

1. The referee declared the fight _____. (adjective)

2. I want to paint my room _____. (adjective)

3. The principal's decision left us _____. (adjective)

4. Our social club elected Mickey _____. (noun)

5. To tell the truth, I found him _____. (adjective)

6. The committee appointed her _____. (noun)

7. For a present I would give them a _____. (noun)

8. Label all the packages _____. (adjective)

9. If it were up to me, I'd call the baby _____. (noun)

10. Yes, we made Tommy _____. (noun)

18.3 Objective Complements • Practice 2

Objective Complements

▶ **Exercise 1** **Using Objective Complements.** Write the sentences, adding appropriate objective complements of the types indicated in parentheses.

EXAMPLE: My best friend calls me (noun). ___*My best friend calls me her trusted advisor.*___

1. My grandfather thinks me (adjective).

   _____

2. Yesterday, the committee appointed Harold (noun).

   _____

3. The Board of Trustees named the new building (noun).

   _____

4. The critics called the star (adjective) and (adjective).

   _____

5. I consider my dog (noun).

   _____

6. The community elected Mr Whipple (noun).

   _____

7. The buttermilk makes the cake (adjective) and (adjective).

   _____

8. I hereby designate this spot (noun).

   _____

9. I labeled the container (noun).

   _____

10. Pat nominated herself (noun).

   _____

▶ **Exercise 2** **Writing Sentences with Direct Objects and Objective Complements.** For each given subject, complete a sentence that includes both a direct object and an objective complement. Then circle the direct object and underline the objective complement.

EXAMPLE: The enthusiastic teacher called her (students) brilliant.

1. The inexperienced waiter _____

2. The hungry lion _____

3. The tiny kitten _____

4. One brave mountain-climber _____

5. One talented ballerina _____

6. A silly juggler _____

7. The committee members _____

8. Two world leaders _____

9. The judges _____

10. The baseball team _____

18.3 Subject Complements • Practice 1

Subject Complements   A subject complement is a noun, pronoun, or adjective that follows a linking verb and tells something about the subject. There are two kinds of subject complements. A predicate nominative is a noun or pronoun that renames or identifies the subject. A predicate adjective is an adjective that describes the subject.

```
                    SUBJECT COMPLEMENTS

                                            PN
Predicate Nominative: James is our new captain.
                          =
                                      PA
Predicate Adjective: James is very intelligent.
                        =
```

▶ **Exercise 1**   **Recognizing Predicate Nominatives and Predicate Adjectives.**   Underline the predicate nominatives and predicate adjectives. Next to each sentence, write either *PN* (predicate nominative) or *PA* (predicate adjective).

EXAMPLE: My baby sister is <u>beautiful</u>.   *PA*

1. Julie is our representative on the Student Council. _____
2. Suddenly, the sky seems threatening. _____
3. Sam became our captain in his senior year. _____
4. Of all cities, Los Angeles is the most polyglot. _____
5. Jean remained our secretary for two terms. _____
6. She is highly susceptible to colds. _____
7. My favorite sport is basketball. _____
8. The book you want is an almanac. _____
9. The senator often appears tired. _____
10. Since the accident, Mother sometimes looks sad. _____

▶ **Exercise 2**   **Writing Sentences with Predicate Nominatives or Predicate Adjectives.**   Fill in the blanks in each sentence with the kind of subject complement listed.

EXAMPLE: Chris was elected _____*secretary*_____. (predicate nominative)

1. Our new car is very _____. (predicate adjective)
2. Next year, Phil will be our _____. (predicate nominative)
3. My favorite day is _____. (predicate nominative)
4. Father sounded quite _____. (predicate adjective)
5. Cary Grant is a famous _____. (predicate nominative)
6. The library was totally _____. (predicate adjective)
7. The capital of our state is _____. (predicate nominative)
8. My old room was more _____. (predicate adjective)
9. The most pleasant season is _____. (predicate nominative)
10. Your new boots are _____. (predicate adjective)

18.3 Subject Complements • Practice 2

Subject Complements

▶ **Exercise 1** **Identifying Subject Complements.** Underline the subject complement in each sentence, including all parts of any compound subject complements. Then identify each as a *predicate nominative* or *predicate adjective*.

EXAMPLE: After the game the team looked exhausted. _predicate adjective_

1. Despite the frost, the fruit trees remained healthy. _____

2. The student will become either an accountant or a banker. _____

3. The blister grew more painful. _____

4. The house looked a mess after the party. _____

5. Through the early morning mist, the foghorn sounded mournful and distant.

6. Cockroaches are pests in many households. _____

7. The man seems a competent violinist. _____

8. Suddenly, the noise grew louder. _____

9. The numbers on the calculator appeared faint. _____

10. At the beginning of the race the competitors felt exuberant and confident. _____

▶ **Writing Application** **Using Complements in Your Own Writing.** Write a paragraph or two describing a memorable incident in your life and explaining why it is meaningful to you. Use and label each of the five kinds of complements at least once.

_____

_____

_____

_____

_____

_____

_____

_____

_____

_____

_____

_____

_____

_____

_____

_____

_____

_____

_____

_____

_____

_____

_____

_____

18.3 Reviewing Basic Sentence Patterns
• Practice 1

Five Basic Patterns with Complements   In the English language, subjects, verbs, and complements follow five basic sentence patterns.

SENTENCE PATTERNS WITH ACTION VERBS	
Patterns	**Examples**
S-AV-DO	Father often reads two [newspapers] . (DO)
S-AV-IO-DO	Sheila told [them] (IO) the [news] (DO) .
S-AV-DO-OC	Ted painted the [fence] (DO) [yellow] (OC) .
SENTENCE PATTERNS WITH LINKING VERBS	
S-LV-PN	Charles Wiston is our [ambassador] (PN) .
S-LV-PA	Your mushroom quiche is [delicious] (PA) .

▶ **Exercise 1**   **Recognizing the Parts of Basic Sentence Patterns.**   Underline each subject once and each verb twice. Draw a box around each complement.

EXAMPLE: I gave [Lois] her [present] .

1. Billy bought some cookies at the market.

2. Ottawa is the capital of Canada.

3. Mrs. Williams gave them complete instructions.

4. I always order steak rare.

5. Unfortunately, these melons seem soft.

6. I described our proposed trip to my parents.

7. At the end of the term I offered Beth my notes.

8. I am the secretary of our class this year.

9. My father considers that politician dangerous.

10. Before the interview I felt insecure.

▶ **Exercise 2**   **Recognizing Basic Sentence Patterns.**   Write the pattern of each sentence in Exercise 1.

EXAMPLE: _____S-AV-IO-DO_____

1. _____   6. _____

2. _____   7. _____

3. _____   8. _____

4. _____   9. _____

5. _____   10. _____

18.3 **Reviewing Basic Sentence Patterns**
• Practice 2
Five Basic Patterns with Complements

▶ **Exercise 1**   **Identifying Sentence Patterns.**   In each of the following sentences, underline each subject once, underline each verb twice, and circle each complement. Then write the pattern of each sentence using abbreviations.

1. The breakfast cook scrambled my eggs. _____

2. The men and women in the audience laughed heartily. _____

3. I named my new car Otto. _____

4. The toddler looked happy and well fed. _____

5. She is the star of that movie. _____

6. Puppies are good pets for children. _____

7. We made the deserted house clean and habitable. _____

8. After hours of hard work, I promised myself a restful midday break. _____

9. Skunks smell offensive to most people. _____

10. Today we washed the windows and vacuumed the rugs. _____

11. Keesha performed her role competently. _____

12. The pizza gave me a stomachache. _____

13. The announcer called the quarterback's play dangerous. _____

14. The unruly guest made the host nervous. _____

15. Sylvia's experiment was daring. _____

▶ **Exercise 2**   **Writing Sentences with Patterns.**   Write a sentence having the pattern indicated in parentheses.

EXAMPLE: (S-AV-IO-DO)   _Marsha bought herself some new boots._

    Key of Pattern Abbreviations
        S-AV-DO = Subject-Action Verb-Direct Object
        S-AV-IO-DO = Subject-Action Verb-Indirect Object-Direct Object
        S-AV-DO-OC = Subject-Action Verb-Direct Object-Objective Complement
        S-LV-PN = Subject-Linking Verb-Predicate Nominative
        S-LV-PA = Subject-Linking Verb-Predicate Adjective

1. (S-AV-DO) _____

2. (S-AV-IO-DO) _____

3. (S-AV-DO-OC) _____

4. (S-LV-PN) _____

5. (S-LV-PA) _____

6. (S-AV-DO) _____

7. (S-AV-IO-DO) _____

8. (S-AV-DO-OC) _____

9. (S-LV-PN) _____

10. (S-LV-PA) _____

18.3 # Reviewing Basic Inverted Sentence Patterns • **Practice 1**

Inverted Patterns   In an inverted sentence pattern, the subject is never first.

PATTERNS IN INVERTED QUESTIONS	
Patterns	**Examples**
V-S	Where is Frank?
HV-S-V	Has Mary arrived yet?
COMP-HV-S-V	What color have you chosen? (DO)

PATTERNS INVERTED FOR EMPHASIS	
V-S	Through the sky streaked the jet.
COMP-S-V	What a difficult time we had! (DO)
COMP-V-S	How long was the wait! (PA)

▶ **Exercise 1**   **Identifying Inverted Sentence Patterns.**   Underline each subject once and each verb twice. Draw a box around each complement. Then the write pattern of each sentence.

EXAMPLE: Did Bill bring his wife ?   _HV-S-V-COMP_

1. Is Frank coming home? _____

2. Toward the schooner moved the Coast Guard cutter. _____

3. Did Marcia win her match? _____

4. Away from the dock raced the boat. _____

5. Here is my friend. _____

6. What movie did you see? _____

7. What a good time we had at the party! _____

8. What books have you read? _____

9. Was Aram happy? _____

10. How wonderful was the play! _____

▶ **Exercise 2**   **Writing Inverted Sentences.**   Use each pattern below in a sentence of your own.

1. HV-S-V _____

2. COMP-V-S _____

3. V-S _____

4. COMP-HV-S-V _____

5. COMP-S-V _____

6. COMP-HV-S-V _____

7. COMP-V-S _____

8. HV-S-V-COMP _____

9. HV-S-V _____

10. COMP-HV-S-V _____

18.3 Reviewing Basic Inverted Sentence Patterns • Practice 2

Inverted Patterns

▶ **Exercise 1** **Identifying Inverted Sentence Patterns.** In each of the following sentences, underline each subject once, underline each verb twice, and circle each complement. Then write the pattern of each sentence using abbreviations.

EXAMPLE: Did Alice remember (you)? _____ *HV-S-V-COMP*

1. What crops did the farmer plant? _____

2. Here is your lunch. _____

3. How angry I am! _____

4. Did John telephone? _____

5. Is the baby asleep? _____

6. Did you read this book? _____

7. At the end of the leash pranced and barked a tiny dog. _____

8. Are Susan and Linda cleaning their rooms? _____

9. Is Kevin at wrestling practice? _____

10. How crowded the store was! _____

▶ **Writing Application** **Writing Sentences with a Variety of Patterns.** Use each pattern in a sentence of your own. Then underline each subject once, underline each verb twice, and circle each complement.

1. S-AV-DO _____

2. HV-S-V-COMP _____

3. S-AV-IO-DO _____

4. S-AV-DO-OC _____

5. S-LV-PN _____

6. COMP-S-V _____

7. S-S-AV-DO-OC-DO-OC _____

8. S-AV-IO-IO-DO _____

9. S-LV-PA-LV-PA _____

10. S-S-AV-IO-DO-AV-DO-OC _____

19.1 Prepositional Phrases • Practice 1

Prepositional Phrases   A phrase is a group of words, without a subject and verb, that is used in a sentence as one part of speech. An adjective phrase is a prepositional phrase that modifies a noun or pronoun by telling what kind or which one.

> **ADJECTIVE PHRASES**
>
> The book jacket *on that novel* is attractive. (*Which* book jacket?)
>
> She wore a coat *of fine alpaca*. (*What* kind of coat?)

An adverb phrase is a prepositional phrase that modifies a verb, adjective, or adverb by pointing out where, when, in what manner, or to what extent.

> **ADVERB PHRASES**
>
> *In the bus* she began to cry. (Began *where*?)
>
> Alex was very happy *about the raise*. (Happy to *what extent*?)
>
> She worked *on Tuesday*. (Worked *when*?)

▶ **Exercise 1**   **Identifying Adjective and Adverb Phrases.**   Underline each prepositional phrase in the sentences below. Then circle the word or words each phrase modifies and label the phrase *adjective* or *adverb*.

EXAMPLE: I watched the frightened (rabbit) in the thicket. _____*adjective*_____

1. In the morning I moved the trash boxes. _____
2. My parents arrived early for the party. _____
3. The room in the attic has been opened recently. _____
4. Years ago we often strolled on the boardwalk. _____
5. The hotels in Atlantic City are large and ornate. _____
6. With a quick wave, he signaled the acrobats. _____
7. I remember the man with a raspy voice. _____
8. The children were hungry after the game. _____
9. At the station we all waited patiently. _____
10. The box with the yellow bow is her present. _____

▶ **Exercise 2**   **Writing Sentences with Adjective and Adverb Phrases.**   Write phrases to complete the following sentences. Then label each phrase as *adjective* or *adverb*.

EXAMPLE: The books I needed were piled _____*on the floor*_____ . ___*adverb*___

1. The water _____ is polluted. _____
2. Chris left _____ . _____
3. _____ , Father drove Kim to Boston. _____
4. The sign _____ annoys me. _____
5. I often study _____ . _____

19.1 Prepositional Phrases • Practice 2

▷ **Exercise 1**   **Identifying Adjective and Adverb Phrases.**   Underline the prepositional phrase or phrases contained in each sentence. Then identify each phrase as *adjective* or *adverb*.

EXAMPLE: The study of animals is fascinating.   *adjective*

(1) A well known theory is the theory of the survival of the fittest. _____

(2) It states that either animals adapt to their environment or they perish from it. _____ (3) The anteater with its almost laughable appearance is one beast that has adapted extremely well. _____ (4) These animals, which live throughout Central and South America, exist almost solely on ants and termites. _____

(5) The anteater's snout can smell the insects from a distance of twenty feet. _____ (6) Since the beasts suffer from nearsightedness, this highly developed sense of smell is important to their survival. _____ (7) Furthermore, on their front feet, anteaters are equipped with sharp claws that may grow to four inches in length. _____ (8) With these tools, anteaters dig up and expose anthills and termite nests. _____ (9) Finally, their sticky tongues can be extended over two feet. _____ (10) This helps anteaters consume thirty thousand ants during a single day. _____

▷ **Exercise 2**   **Identifying Adjective and Adverb Phrases.**   Underline the prepositional phrase in each sentence. Then identify it by writing *adjective phrase* or *adverb phrase* in the blank.

EXAMPLE: We yawned on the way out.   *adverb phrase*

1. After an hour, I finally finished the dishes. _____
2. You can make time for anything. _____
3. The lady in the blue socks ran the fastest. _____
4. Inez will take the important test on Friday. _____
5. Jack and Jill climbed up the hill. _____
6. Stella is very excited about her new job. _____
7. An error of ten percent will doom the project. _____
8. The book with the blue cover is very interesting. _____
9. Even now, the scene remains in my mind. _____
10. The team with the green jerseys is ours. _____
11. The coach with the long hair worked the athletes hard. _____
12. Eating an entire pizza with mushrooms and olives was easy. _____
13. Sara sat by the pool and read her novel. _____
14. Your college application form is on the table. _____
15. Safety rules for all workers must be followed strictly. _____

19.1 Appositives • Practice 1

Appositives and Appositive Phrases   An appositive is a noun or pronoun placed next to another noun or pronoun to identify, rename, or explain it.

APPOSITIVE PHRASES
Joe's favorite team, the Giants, won the game.
Ophelia Jones, an actress, spoke at our school.

An appositive phrase is a noun or pronoun with modifiers, placed next to a noun or pronoun to add information and details.

APPOSITIVE PHRASES
Bob's living quarters, *a room in an attic*, would not suit me.
He was the brother of Theda Bara, *a famous silent-screen actress*.

▶ **Exercise 1**   **Identifying Appositives and Appositive Phrases.**   Underline each appositive or appositive phrase in these sentences. Circle the noun or pronoun it renames.

EXAMPLE: (Miss Johnson) , an art teacher, decided to retire.

1. My favorite uncle, a traveling salesman, often visits.
2. I sold my old car, the Rambler.
3. *Newswire*, an afternoon newspaper, has a magazine section.
4. *Gourmet*, a painting by Picasso, shows a little girl eating at a table.
5. My brother Richard is still in college.
6. Today, helicopters, aircraft with whirling rotor blades, are important in military reconnaissance.
7. I would like to introduce Archie Lee, my football coach.
8. Her slippers, open shoes with two straps, were expensive.
9. I stared at her face, a face consumed with heartbreak.
10. We read *Ethan Frome*, a novel by Edith Wharton.

▶ **Exercise 2**   **Writing Sentences with Appositives and Appositive Phrases.**   Turn each pair of sentences into a single sentence by adding one or more appositives or appositive phrases.

EXAMPLE: Her plants are flourishing. They are all ferns.
            Her plants, all ferns, are flourishing.

1. I love boston cream pie. It is a cake made with chocolate and custard.

    _____

2. Her favorite meal will be served today. It is roast chicken.

    _____

3. Trenton is a rapidly changing city. It is the capital of New Jersey.

    _____

4. India is the scene of many of Kipling's stories. It is a land of contrasts.

    _____

5. Most people have never played polo. It is a very expensive game.

    _____

19.1 Appositives • Practice 2

▶ **Exercise 1**   **Identifying Appositives and Appositive Phrases.**   Write each appositive or appositive phrase.

EXAMPLE: My friends Jean and Bob are going with me.   _Jean and Bob_

1. That tent over there, the large one with orange trim, looks right for our

   family. _____

2. Two ports—St. Thomas and Nassau—were lively. _____

3. We served Manhattan clam chowder, a tomato-based soup. _____

4. The couple named the child Miley, an old family name. _____

5. The play, a comedy, kept us laughing all evening. _____

6. The children, not the teenagers, can get reduced air fares. _____

7. The road, really no more than a trail, leads to the cabin. _____

8. I told the two children, Dan and Sue, a story. _____

9. She planted the trees in special soil—a rich compost. _____

10. I eat grapefruit, my favorite breakfast food, every morning. _____

▶ **Exercise 2**   **Using Appositives and Appositive Phrases to Combine Sentences.**   Turn each
pair of sentences into a single sentence with an appositive or appositive phrase.

EXAMPLE: I will ask Beth. She is an excellent student.   _I will ask Beth, an excellent student._

1. Dr. Kirk is retiring this year. She is our family doctor.

   _____

2. Backpackers enjoy hiking into Desolation Valley. It is an uninhabited region filled with hundreds of
   lakes.

   _____

3. The birds sat within a foot of the window. They were wrens.

   _____

4. We visited only three places. They were the Empire State Building, Central Park, and the Statute of
   Liberty.

   _____

5. The king thoroughly enjoyed all seven courses of the royal banquet. He was a rotund little man with

   many chins.

   _____

6. Loosestrife grew by the road. Loosestrife is a wildflower with spikes of white, yellow, rose, or purple
   flowers.

   _____

7. He suffers from acrophobia. Acrophobia is a fear of heights.

   _____

8. I would like you to meet Barbara. She is my cousin.

   _____

9. The shrew is the smallest mammal. A shrew is a mouselike creature with a long snout.

   _____

10. We finally reached the coast. It was a deserted beach.

   _____

Verbal Phrases—Participial Phrases
19.2
• **Practice 1**

Participles and Participial Phrases A verbal is a word derived from a verb but used as a noun, adjective, or adverb. A participle is a form of a verb that can act as an adjective. A participial phrase is a participle that is modified by an adverb or adverb phrase or that has a complement. The entire phrase acts as an adjective in a sentence. Participles and participial phrases have two forms: present and past.

Participles	Participial Phrases
Present: The *winning* player waited on the court.	*Present:* The man *running well* is a pro.
Present: Smiling, she agreed to go with us.	*Present: Smiling at her mother,* she accepted her award.
Past: My *worried* father phoned.	*Past:* The man *told to wait* left through a back door.
Past: Troubled, she spoke to her counselor.	*Past: Chosen as captain,* Bill thanked his teammates.

▶ **Exercise 1** **Identifying Present and Past Participles.** Underline the participle in each sentence and circle the word it modifies. On the line at the right, write *present* or *past* to tell which form it is.

EXAMPLE: Disturbed, (Mother) called the police. _____*past*_____

1. The whining child continued to complain. _____

2. You tried to sell me a broken vase. _____

3. Laughing, she described the humorous incident. _____

4. Did you ever try to fix a damaged engine? _____

5. Dismayed, he walked out of the interview. _____

6. Swollen, the river continued to rise. _____

7. If possible, use a soothing lotion on the wound. _____

8. The speaker is a distinguished statesman. _____

9. A beginning player often has some trouble. _____

10. Swimming, I learned to breathe properly. _____

▶ **Exercise 2** **Identifying Participial Phrases.** Underline each participial phrase and circle the word it modifies.

EXAMPLE: Walking briskly, (I) soon reached the depot.

1. Groping in the dark, Beth finally found her keys.

2. The general, broken in spirit, retired in a matter of months.

3. Chosen by the committee, Alice began to make plans.

4. Painting slowly, he completed the mural in two years.

5. The principal, arriving at seven, opened the building.

6. Abandoned by its owner, the puppy wandered about aimlessly.

7. The famous actress, reached in her dressing room, denied the story.

8. Rinsing the vegetables, he began to prepare the salad.

9. The writer, torn by indecision, destroyed his manuscript.

10. Traveling to Italy, she visited Rome, Florence, and Naples.

19.2 Verbal Phrases—Participial Phrases
• Practice 2

▶ Exercise 1 **Recognizing Participles and Participial Phrases.** Underline each participle or participial phrase. Then indicate if it is *present*, *past*, or *perfect*.

EXAMPLE: The exhausted swimmer finally reached shore. ___past___

1. Expecting good news, the student raced to the mailbox. _____
2. The slouching model soon found herself out of a job. _____
3. The key witness, protected by two guards, has arrived. _____
4. I, having auditioned yesterday, waited for the results. _____
5. The soccer players, having grown faint from thirst, gratefully accepted the cold oranges. _____
6. We drink purified water in our home. _____
7. Famished from the exercise, the wrestler ate a whole pizza. _____
8. The chef, having buttered the bread, warmed it in the oven. _____
9. Impeached by the legislature, the politician headed home. _____
10. Hitting the shelf, I almost dislodged the jar of fruit. _____

▶ Exercise 2 **Punctuating Participial Phrases.** Underline each participial phrase. Set off any nonessential participial phrases with commas.

EXAMPLE: This story, first told to me by my grandmother, has always been my favorite.

1. The stars found on the United States flag now total fifty.
2. The White House built on swamp land has sunk a quarter inch in thirty years.
3. A salami weighing 457 pounds was put on exhibit.
4. A cat named Tiger walked over 250 miles to find his family.
5. Calendars first produced by studying the stars now come in a great variety of forms.
6. A dance marathon lasting twenty-five weeks was finally stopped by the authorities.
7. Canada claimed by Cartier for France in 1534 is the second largest country in the world.
8. The Grand Old Opry featuring some of the best country singers attracts visitors from all over the United States.
9. Ships transporting grain and iron ore use the Great Lakes.
10. The highest peak in North America is Mount McKinley located in Alaska.

▶ Exercise 3 **Recognizing Nominative Absolutes.** Underline the subject once, underline the verb twice, and circle the nominative absolute.

1. I collected my roll of film, a week having gone by.
2. The day being too windy, we did not use our umbrellas.
3. I fixed dinner quickly, my stomach growling with hunger.
4. The book being in demand, another printing was ordered.
5. The paint mixed, we dipped our brushes into it.
6. The team having won, we gave a party to celebrate.
7. We swam all day, the temperature being ninety degrees.
8. The lilacs being in bloom, a delightful fragrance filled the air.
9. The car not starting, I looked under the hood.
10. The movie over, I went home to bed.

19.2 Verbal Phrases—Gerund Phrases • Practice 1

Gerunds and Gerund Phrases   A gerund is a form of verb that acts as a noun. A gerund phrase is a gerund with modifiers or complements, all acting together as a noun. Gerunds and gerund phrases can be used as subjects, direct objects, indirect objects, objects of prepositions, predicate nominatives, and appositives.

Gerunds	Gerund Phrases
Subject: *Talking* is not permitted here.	*Subject*: *Growing tall* is a family characteristic.
Direct Object: I always enjoy *laughing*.	*Direct Object*: I like *swimming daily at the pool*.
Predicate Nominative: His favorite sport is *skiing*.	*Object of a Preposition*: He talked about *collecting stamps*.
Appositive: His bad habit, *snoring*, annoyed them all.	*Indirect Object*: During the gas shortage, he gave *walking* to the station a try.

Exercise 1   **Identifying Gerunds and Gerund Phrases.**   Underline the gerund or gerund phrases in each sentence. In the space provided, tell how it is used.

EXAMPLE: I enjoy reading magazines and newspapers. ___*direct object*___

1. Sailing has always been her passion. _____
2. He often writes about growing old. _____
3. Dorene enjoys dancing in bare feet. _____
4. Pam's bad habit, giggling incessantly, now seems under control. _____
5. Developing a new system is Tom's goal. _____
6. Todd gave break dancing a bad name. _____
7. After two miles, she was exhausted from jogging. _____
8. For a while he tried singing with a new band. _____
9. Driving on that road is dangerous. _____
10. Her chief fault is speaking too rapidly. _____

Exercise 2   **Writing Sentences with Gerunds and Gerund Phrases.**   Use the following gerunds and gerund phrases as indicated below.

EXAMPLE: *drinking* as a direct object ___*I avoid drinking too many soft drinks.*___

1. *running fast* as a subject _____
2. *reading* as a direct object _____
3. *telling stories* as an object of a preposition _____
4. *cooking* as a predicate nominative _____
5. *collecting coins* as an appositive _____
6. *swimming* as a subject _____
7. *designing clothes* as a direct object _____
8. *getting help* as an object of a preposition _____
9. *speaking loudly* as a subject _____
10. *playing baseball* as a direct object _____

19.2 Verbal Phrases—Gerund Phrases • Practice 2

▶ **Exercise 1** **Identifying Gerunds and Gerund Phrases.** Underline each gerund or gerund phrase. Then, identify its function as a *subject, direct object, indirect object, object of a preposition, predicate nominative,* or *appositive.*

EXAMPLE: I was tired of waiting on you. ___*object of a preposition*___

1. Trying harder is sometimes the answer. _____
2. I just finished typing my term paper. _____
3. Sally wants a job in banking. _____
4. Playing the piano can be a very satisfying activity. _____
5. Kim has developed her gift, singing, exceptionally well. _____
6. One serious crime for hunters is poaching. _____
7. We finally stopped the bleeding from the cut in her leg. _____
8. When you clean, avoid mixing bleach with ammonia. _____
9. I became ill after eating the spoiled meat. _____
10. The clown's best trick was juggling. _____
11. Sadly, studying has always been difficult for Mason. _____
12. Jack's sister Kate has never enjoyed swimming. _____
13. Kwan was elated after hearing the good news. _____
14. Brian's favorite activity is sleeping. _____
15. Your principal occupation, loafing, will not contribute to your success. _____

▶ **Exercise 2** **Completing Sentences with Gerund Phrases.** Complete each sentence with an appropriate gerund phrase. Then, in the blank following the sentence, write the way in which the gerund phrase is used (*subject, direct object, indirect object, object of a preposition, predicate nominative,* or *appositive*).

EXAMPLE: The singer was famous for ___*hitting very high notes*___ . ___*object of a preposition*___

1. _____ is a very serious mistake. _____
2. Our goal, _____ , seems within easy reach. _____
3. Do you enjoy _____ ? _____
4. Your most important activity today will be _____ . _____
5. Ralph gave _____ a year of his time, but he lost money. _____
6. Wash your hands before _____ . _____
7. _____ on a windy day can be a very enjoyable experience. _____
8. The book has a very interesting title, _____ . _____
9. Have you finished _____ yet? _____
10. Last year, Sally's hobby was _____ . _____
11. Diana dreaded _____ , but she did it anyway. _____
12. _____ is good exercise. _____
13. Carla's favorite exercise, _____ , is Casey's least favorite. _____
14. Running is an effective method for _____ . _____
15. Although he was lost, Raymond was against _____ . _____

19.2 Verbal Phrases—Infinitive Phrases
• Practice 1

Infinitives and Infinitive Phrases An infinitive is a form of a verb that generally appears with the word *to* and acts as a noun, adjective, or adverb. An infinitive phrase is an infinitive with modifiers, a complement, or a subject, all acting together as a single part of speech.

Infinitives	Infinitive Phrases
Subject: *To win* is our goal.	Subject: *To learn London* was her first objective.
Direct Object: She wants *to leave.*	Direct Object: We watched *him sail out of the harbor.*
Adjective: This is the one *to buy.*	Adjective: The best route *to take to Canton* is the old route.
Adverb: This is easy *to do.*	Adverb: The team fought *to get the ball back.*

▶ **Exercise 1** **Identifying Infinitives and Infinitive Phrases.** Underline the infinitive or the infinitive phrase in each sentence. In the space provided, tell whether the infinitive or infinitive phrase is used as a *noun, adverb,* or *adjective*.

EXAMPLE: This is difficult to do. _____adverb_____

1. To drive well is one of my desires. _____

2. Of course, she is happy to go. _____

3. Here are the instructions to get to the museum. _____

4. I think the rules are easy to follow. _____

5. Phil left to catch his train. _____

6. She said she would like to rest a bit. _____

7. His daily goal, to jog, is not always possible. _____

8. We expected to fly to Los Angeles yesterday. _____

9. Yes, the mayor is about to speak. _____

10. It is simple to follow these directions. _____

▶ **Exercise 2** **Writing Sentences with Infinitives and Infinitive Phrases.** Use the following infinitives and infinitive phrases as directed.

EXAMPLE: *to see* as an adverb _____The statue was hard to see._____

1. *to read three books* as a subject _____

2. *to do* as an adverb _____

3. *to walk* as a direct object _____

4. *to learn* as an adjective _____

5. *to go* as an object of a preposition _____

6. *to eat lunch* as a direct object _____

7. *to work* as a subject _____

8. *to freeze* as an adverb _____

9. *to watch* as an adjective _____

10. *to react quickly* as a direct object _____

19.2 **Verbal Phrases—Infinitive Phrases**
• Practice 2

▶ **Exercise 1** **Identifying Infinitives and Infinitive Phrases.** Underline each infinitive or infinitive phrase. Then, label each as a *subject, direct object, predicate nominative, object of preposition, appositive, adjective,* or *adverb.*

EXAMPLE: To win at chess requires concentration. ___*subject*___

1. The magician's best trick was to disappear in a teacup. _____
2. The doctor was known for his ability to perform surgery. _____
3. The bus to Houston is about to depart. _____
4. The future is often unpleasant to contemplate. _____
5. I watched the soccer team play. _____
6. I dared not interrupt the judge. _____
7. The wrestler was glad to win the match. _____
8. My friend bought a new coat to wear to the opera. _____
9. He was happy to have been the center of attention. _____
10. Let us go to the movies tonight. _____
11. To plan a wonderful party is not the easiest task. _____
12. Would you like to see the week-old kittens? _____
13. Tim was practicing daily to improve his skills. _____
14. Sue had hoped to participate in the event. _____
15. The best place to get fresh vegetables is from your own garden. _____

▶ **Writing Application** **Writing Sentences with Verbals.** Use each of the following verbs in three sentences—first as a participle, then as a gerund, and finally as an infinitive. Underline the verbal or verbal phrase in each sentence.

EXAMPLE: cook *I prefer cooked mushrooms to raw ones.*
Cooking is my favorite pastime.
Steaming is the best way to cook vegetables.

1. run _____
_____
_____

2. dance _____
_____
_____

3. live _____
_____
_____

4. grow _____
_____
_____

5. open _____
_____
_____

19.3 Clauses • Practice 1

A clause is a group of words with its own subject and verb. There are two kinds. An independent clause can stand by itself as a complete sentence. A subordinate clause cannot stand by itself as a complete sentence.

Adjective Clauses   An adjective clause is a subordinate clause that modifies a noun or pronoun by telling what kind or which one. Adjective clauses begin with relative pronouns or relative adverbs.

ADJECTIVE CLAUSES
I bought the book *which was on sale.*
The man *whom you described* is my uncle.
We need a place *where we can relax.*

Relative pronouns act as nouns or adjectives within the adjective clauses. Relative adverbs act as adverbs within the clauses. Note that in some sentences, such as the last one below, a relative pronoun may be understood.

THE USE OF RELATIVE PRONOUNS
The woman who *visited us* is brilliant. (subject)
The man whose *car is outside* will be disappointed. (adjective)
This is the magazine (that) *we need.* (understood direct object)

▶ **Exercise 1**   **Identifying Adjective Clauses.**   Underline the adjective clause and circle the noun or pronoun it modifies.

EXAMPLE: I know the (girl) who wrote to you.

1. The book that you mentioned is no longer in print.
2. It is they who should be ashamed.
3. The capital which we visited is not a very big city.
4. This is the style that she prefers.
5. The man whom you spoke to is the general manager.
6. Is this the map which he wanted?
7. An apartment that faces south is often expensive.
8. I tried to match the color that she described.
9. The governor whose face was most familiar was Governor Chase.
10. We opened the chest which they had spent so much for.

▶ **Exercise 2**   **Identifying the Use of Relative Pronouns.**   Identify the use within the subordinate clause of each of the pronouns in Exercise 1. A pronoun can be used as *subject, direct object, object of a preposition,* or *adjective.*

EXAMPLE: I know the (girl) who wrote to you. ____subject____

1. _____   6. _____
2. _____   7. _____
3. _____   8. _____
4. _____   9. _____
5. _____   10. _____

19.3 Adjective Clauses • Practice 2

Exercise 1 **Identifying Adjective Clauses.** Underline the adjective clause in each sentence, circling the relative pronoun or relative adverb. Then label the use of the circled word within the clause as *subject, direct object, objective of a preposition, adjective,* or *adverb.*

EXAMPLE: He returned the book (that) he borrowed. ____*direct object*____

1. My parents prefer a radio station that plays nothing but classical music. _____

2. The white shark that was caught had to be released. _____

3. I met the author whose book I just read. _____

4. The place where the meeting was held was too small. _____

5. The political issue on which the argument centered seemed trivial. _____

6. Dr. Bower, whom the community respects, has retired. _____

7. I used the pen that still had plenty of ink. _____

8. You should know the reason why he scolded you. _____

9. My neighbor, the woman whose house is filled with valuable antiques, is planning to have a garage sale. _____

10. The chicken that I roasted was delicious. _____

11. The Andersons live in the house that their grandfather built. _____

12. Darla is the girl who always arrives early. _____

13. My bicycle, which I bought two years ago, needs new brakes. _____

14. This is one time when you will have to make a sacrifice. _____

15. She is the woman who works at the bank. _____

Exercise 2 **Writing Sentences with Adjective Clauses.** For each item, write a sentence that uses the adjective clause in parentheses. Then circle the word that the adjective clause modifies.

EXAMPLE: (whom you recognized) That (man) whom you recognized at the bazaar is standing over there by the pool.

1. (who live on that street) _____

2. (which includes a free prize) _____

3. (that I earned last summer) _____

4. (whom you met last week) _____

5. (when Alice arrived at the station) _____

6. (where the class had its annual picnic) _____

7. (why we were unable to succeed) _____

8. (who hosted the open house) _____

9. (which costs only ten dollars) _____

10. (that you asked for) _____

11. (whom Peter told you about) _____

12. (when the fans jumped to their feet) _____

13. (where the swans glide peacefully all day) _____

14. (why Caroline was eager to contribute) _____

15. (who created this game) _____

19.3 Adverb Clauses • Practice 1

Adverb Clauses   Subordinate adverb clauses modify verbs, adjectives, adverbs, or verbals by telling where, when, in what manner, to what extent, under what condition, or why. Adverb clauses are introduced by subordinating conjunctions, such as *although, since, if, when, while,* and *where.*

ADVERB CLAUSES	
Modified Word	**Example**
Verb	*If they arrive early,* we will go to the beach.
Adjective	She was edgy *before she went into the interview.*
Adverb	The parade began sooner *than we expected.*
Verbal	They like to exercise *whenever they can.*

▶ **Exercise 1**   **Identifying Adverb Clauses.**   Underline the adverb clause in each sentence. Circle the word or words it modifies.

EXAMPLE: <u>Since you asked me,</u> I ⟨have received⟩ two other invitations.

1. She is happy whenever she hears from you.

2. Although I still visit this city often, I prefer Denver.

3. To travel whenever you like is a luxury few have.

4. I received a reply faster than I expected.

5. We will take them to the station if they will wait an hour.

6. I try to listen whenever the President speaks.

7. The witness, crying as she spoke, obviously affected the jury.

8. Your act will be first because you are the most skilled.

9. She is upset if she doesn't exercise daily.

10. After she missed the appointment, I spoke to the dentist.

▶ **Exercise 2**   **Writing Sentences with Adverb Clauses.**   Add an appropriate adverb clause to each independent clause below.

EXAMPLE: _____*When everyone had arrived*_____ , we began the party.

1. _____, I will save a seat for you.

2. The storm broke _____.

3. Smiling _____, the audience applauded wildly.

4. I was delighted _____.

5. _____, he took out the trash.

6. She is faster _____

7. I like to swim _____.

8. _____, I tried to reach them.

9. Your room will be ready _____.

10. _____, you will find everyone receptive.

19.3 Adverb Clauses • Practice 2

Exercise 1 **Identifying Adverb Clauses.** Underline the adverb clause in each sentence. Then indicate whether it modifies a *verb, adjective, adverb,* or *verbal.*

EXAMPLE: Although we hurried, we missed the train. ____*verb*____

1. The President waited until he had heard the reports. _____

2. After the mayor cut the ribbon, she entered the park. _____

3. The forest muffled all outside noises when I stood in it. _____

4. To discuss problems whenever they arise is a good policy. _____

5. The turtle crawled slowly as though it were exhausted. _____

6. Eating before I exercise makes me sluggish. _____

7. They will cancel the concert unless more tickets are sold. _____

8. The man, straining as he lifted the piano, injured his back. _____

9. I was glad that my mother agreed with my plan. _____

10. To talk after you are told to stop is to risk punishment. _____

Exercise 2 **Recognizing Elliptical Clauses.** Underline the elliptical adverb clause in each sentence, placing a caret (^) where the understood words belong. Then write the understood word on the line.

EXAMPLE: Maggie wants to go more than I^. ____*do*____

1. The company pays Mr. Hilton more than Mr. Gurney. _____

2. Students often do not know as much about art as adults. _____

3. You play card games better than Vic. _____

4. The nurse is not as qualified as the doctor. _____

5. The wood shop teachers help Allison more than me. _____

6. They are as tired as we. _____

7. A St. Bernard is larger than a German Shepherd. _____

8. He plays more tennis than golf. _____

9. Saudi Arabia has more oil than most other countries. _____

10. You may feel better on a clear day than a rainy one. _____

19.3 # Noun Clauses • **Practice 1**

Noun Clauses   A noun clause is a subordinate clause that acts as a noun.

USES OF NOUN CLAUSES	
Use	**Example**
Subject	*Whomever you choose* will be our representative.
Direct Object	I wonder *how they plan to go.*
Indirect Object	She will give *whomever asks* directions to the stadium.
Object of a Preposition	Fortunately, he usually talks about *what he knows best.*
Predicate Nominative	A good film with lots of action is *what my father prefers.*
Appositive	His suggestion, *that parents fly separately,* has much to recommend it.

▶ **Exercise 1**   **Identifying Noun Clauses.**   Underline the noun clause in each sentence and tell how it is used.

EXAMPLE: I know <u>what they can do</u>.   <u> *direct object* </u>

1. This news is just about what I expected. _____

2. My idea, that the project be postponed, was accepted. _____

3. How this business manages to survive is anyone's guess. _____

4. Do you like what they suggest? _____

5. She gave whoever called both messages. _____

6. I can't imagine how they can go. _____

7. A rigid diet is what Mother needs. _____

8. Whatever price they ask is probably too much. _____

9. I disagree with his proposal that we build another mall. _____

10. The speaker will arrive at whatever time you say. _____

▶ **Exercise 2**   **Writing Sentences with Noun Clauses.**   Add a noun clause to each sentence below.

EXAMPLE: ____*How they will succeed*____ is a mystery to most of us.

1. I wonder _____.

2. We told them about _____.

3. I will give _____ two tickets to the concert.

4. _____ will be our speaker.

5. His idea, _____ is really not possible.

6. She can tell _____.

7. A well-organized chairperson is _____.

8. _____ is something we haven't solved yet.

9. My father cannot decide _____.

10. This is about _____.

19.3 Noun Clauses • Practice 2

Exercise 1 **Identifying Noun Clauses.** Underline the noun clause in each sentence, indicating whether the clause is functioning as a *subject*, *direct object*, *indirect object*, *object of a preposition*, *predicate nominative*, or *appositive*.

(1) The question, how you should choose a college, is a difficult one. _____

(2) You may first look for a college that offers whatever course of study you wish to pursue. _____ (3) Which section of the country a college is in should be considered also. _____ (4) Try to pick a school in whatever climate you will be most comfortable. _____ (5) How close the school is to your home is important. _____ (6) What schools your friends choose may also be important. _____ (7) Another factor is whether the college is in a city or a small town. _____ (8) Rural and urban areas offer whoever resides there different types of activities and resources. _____ (9) Your choice may depend upon how much you can afford to spend for your education. _____ (10) Whom a college decides to accept as a student may prove to be the decisive factor in your choice. _____

Exercise 2 **Identifying Subordinate Clauses.** Identify each underlined clause as *adjective*, *adverb*, or *noun*.

1. Take the layout to the printer who gives the best price. _____
2. When the holiday season begins, the stores are jammed with frantic shoppers. _____
3. Whoever wants a ride to the store had better go to the car. _____
4. Frankenstein's monster, which Mary Shelley first envisioned in a dream in 1816, is often thought to symbolize the outcast in society. _____
5. Daydreaming when I should be working is a problem. _____

Writing Application **Using Subordinate Clauses to Combine Sentences.** Turn each pair of sentences into one by changing one of the sentences into type of clause indicated. Underline each subordinate clause.

EXAMPLE: Combine using an adjective clause: The turkey smelled delicious. We were having it for dinner.
The turkey we were having for dinner smelled delicious.

1. Combine using an adjective clause: Robert Frost wrote "Stopping by Woods on a Snowy Evening." He also wrote many other poems, such as the "The Death of a Hired Man."

   _____

2. Combine using an adverb clause: The farmer milked the cows. Then, she checked on the pigs.

   _____

3. Combine using a noun clause: Someone will get the scholarship. This will be determined by the faculty.

   _____

4. Combine using an adverb clause: The music went faster. I could not sing along that fast.

   _____

5. Combine using an adjective clause: I opened a new book. The book felt crisp and clean to my touch.

   _____

19.4 Sentences Classified by Structure
• Practice 1

The Four Structures of Sentences   English sentences may be classified by the number and kind of clauses they contain.

Kind of Sentence	Number and Kind of Clauses	Examples
Simple	One independent clause	An unusual <u>event</u> <u>occurred</u> twice last month.
Compound	Two or more independent clauses	<u>I</u> <u>know</u> the main highways well, but <u>I</u> usually <u>get</u> lost on the side roads. We often <u>visit</u> the Poconos; sometimes, <u>we</u> <u>stay</u> a full week.
Complex	One independent clause and one or more subordinate clauses	When <u>I</u> <u>travel</u> to the Atlantic Provinces, <u>I</u> <u>hope</u> to visit Nova Scotia and New Brunswick.
Compound-Complex	Two or more independent clauses and one or more subordinate clauses	Since <u>I</u> <u>am</u> ready to begin, <u>I</u> <u>will</u> <u>outline</u> the project, and <u>Ted</u> <u>will</u> <u>give</u> you the details.

▶ **Exercise 1**   **Identifying the Structure of Sentences.**   Identify each sentence as (1) simple, (2) compound, (3) complex, or (4) compound-complex.

EXAMPLE: I will attend or I will send someone. _____2_____

1. All the roads will be flooded unless the storm abates soon. _____

2. My older sister drives, but my younger one has yet to learn. _____

3. My night school class is crowded now, but it will diminish in size as soon as winter comes. _____

4. I prefer roomy American-made cars; my brother likes foreign models. _____

5. Have you completed all your research on the dangers of smoking? _____

6. Since I left, the town has changed greatly. _____

7. Did you buy the cake today, or will you get it later? _____

8. This is the book which I have been trying to get. _____

9. When the economic situation changes, I will sell my old house, and I will buy another closer to the city. _____

10. At the end of the road near the hill is a modern gas station. _____

▶ **Exercise 2**   **Writing Different Types of Sentences.**   Follow the directions below.

1. Write a complex sentence in which the subordinate clause comes first.

_____

2. Write a compound sentence punctuated with a semicolon.

_____

3. Write a sentence in the form of a question.

_____

4. Write a compound-complex sentence consisting of two independent clauses and two subordinate clauses.

_____

Name _____ Date _____

 19.4 # Sentences Classified by Structure
• Practice 2

Exercise 1 ▶ **Identifying the Four Structures of Sentences.** Identify each sentence as *simple, compound, complex,* or *compound-complex*.

EXAMPLE: Forests have supplied people with important products since the earliest times. ___*simple*___

(1) In the world today, most wood is used for fuel, but in the United States most cellulose or plant fiber from trees is used for making paper or paperboard. _____ (2) Lumber or boards, which are cut from logs, are used for making buildings, furniture, musical instruments, caskets, and other important products. _____ (3) Round timbers serve as utility poles and bridge and building supports. _____ (4) Is there anyone who has not used pencils, baseball bats, or toothpicks made of wood? _____ (5) When we ride on trains, the ties supporting the tracks are made of wood, and when doctors examine us, the tongue depressors they use are wooden ones. _____ (6) The charcoal that we use in our grills is heat-treated wood. _____ (7) Acetate and rayon fabrics are made from wood, and even artificial vanilla is made from wood. _____ (8) Forests provide us with nuts and maple syrup. _____ (9) Without forests many species of wildlife would have no homes or food, and we would find it difficult to survive as well. _____ (10) We must be concerned about conserving and replacing our forests, for wherever we look, forest products are playing an important role in our lives. _____

Writing Application ▶ **Writing Sentences with Different Structures.** Use the instructions below to write ten sentences of your own. Then underline each subordinate clause.

1. Write a simple sentence.

   _____

2. Write a simple sentence with a compound verb.

   _____

3. Write a simple sentence containing a verbal phrase.

   _____

4. Write a compound sentence in which the clauses are joined with a conjunction.

   _____

5. Write a compound sentence in which the clauses are joined by a semicolon.

   _____

6. Write a complex sentence with an adverb.

   _____

7. Write a complex sentence with an adjective clause and an adverb clause.

   _____

8. Write a complex sentence with a noun clause.

   _____

9. Write a compound-complex sentence with an adverb clause.

   _____

10. Write a compound-complex sentence with two subordinate clauses.

    _____

60 • Grammar Exercise Workbook   © Prentice-Hall, Inc.

20.1 The Four Functions of Sentences • Practice 1

The Four Functions of Sentences   There are four sentence types: declarative, interrogative, imperative, and exclamatory. A declarative sentence states an idea and ends with a period; an interrogative sentence asks a question and ends with a question mark; an imperative sentence gives an order or direction and ends with a period or exclamation mark; an exclamatory sentence conveys strong emotion and ends with an exclamation mark.

FOUR FUNCTIONS OF SENTENCES
Declarative: Emiliano Zapata, the Mexican peasant leader, died in 1919.
Interrogative: When did Marie Curie first win the Nobel Prize?
Imperative: Harvest the apple crop next week.
Exclamatory: What an unexpected tragedy this is!

▶ Exercise 1   **Identifying the Four Functions of Sentences.**   Identify each sentence as *declarative, interrogative, imperative,* or *exclamatory.* Also place the proper punctuation mark at the end of each sentence.

EXAMPLE: When was the Empire State Building constructed.
        When was the Empire State Building constructed ___?___   *interrogative*

1. How dreadful that sounds _____

2. The inner walls have begun to crumble _____

3. How much did your new stereo cost _____

4. Pay close attention _____

5. Which President followed Grover Cleveland _____

6. The Danube is the second largest river in Europe _____

7. What a dangerous hurricane _____

8. Try on another pair of shoes _____

9. Who wrote Ethan Frome _____

10. The Matterhorn is located in the Swiss Pennine Alps _____

▶ Exercise 2   **Writing Original Sentences.**   Complete the work below.

1. Write two declarative sentences.

   _____

   _____

2. Write two interrogative sentences.

   _____

   _____

3. Write three imperative sentences.

   _____

   _____

   _____

4. Write three exclamatory sentences.

   _____

   _____

   _____

20.1 The Four Functions of Sentences • Practice 2

▶ **Exercise 1** **Identifying the Four Functions of Sentences.** Identify each sentence as *declarative*, *interrogative*, *imperative*, or *exclamatory*. Then write the end mark for each sentence.

EXAMPLE: What an incredible story that was ___exclamatory !___

1. This area gets poor television reception _____
2. Do you want to leave Friday morning or afternoon _____
3. This is ridiculous _____
4. My friend does not care for diet drinks _____
5. When will the loan be ready _____
6. Fill the car with gas on your way home _____
7. I wonder where my turtle has gone _____
8. Ask Mindy to stop by after school _____
9. The sunset cast a rosy glow on the walls of the building _____
10. Would you pass me the hammer _____

▶ **Exercise 2** **Writing Sentences with Different Functions.** Write a sentence for each number, using the subject and function indicated. For example, the first sentence should be a *declarative* sentence about *wild animals*.

	Declarative	Interrogative	Imperative	Exclamatory
Wild Animals	1	2	3	4
Holidays	5	6	7	8
School Activities	9	10	11	12

1. _____
2. _____
3. _____
4. _____
5. _____
6. _____
7. _____
8. _____
9. _____
10. _____
11. _____
12. _____

20.2 Sentence Combining • Practice 1

Sentence Combining   Combine short, related sentences by using compound subjects or verbs, phrases, or compound, complex, or compound-complex sentences.

Short Sentences	Combined Sentences
The team won the game. They moved into first place.	The team won the game and moved into first place.
Ann overslept this morning. She was late for school.	Because Ann overslept this morning, she was late for school.
Brent went out for the evening. He left the stove on. His house burned down.	When Brent went out for the evening, he left the stove on, and his house burned down.

▶ **Exercise 1**   **Combining Sentences.**   Combine the sentences in each item into a single sentence.

EXAMPLE: Chico is a good student. He is also a gifted athlete.

_____ *Chico is a good student and a gifted athlete.* _____

1. Sandy skied into a pine tree. She broke her leg. _____

_____

2. The police car had its siren blaring and its lights flashing. It raced to the scene of the crime. _____

_____

3. I saw Dudley at the library. He looked tired. _____

_____

4. It has been snowing for two days. All the roads are closed. _____

_____

5. The President felt ill this morning. His speech was canceled. _____

_____

▶ **Exercise 2**   **More Work with Sentence Combining.**   Follow the directions in Exercise 1.

1. Abalone is prized for its delicate meat. It is also valued for the mother-of-pearl lining of its shell. It is found only on the Pacific coast of North America. _____

_____

2. Roger went to the concert last night. He met a girl there whom he liked. He asked her to go out with him after the show. _____

_____

3. Few people volunteered. Those of us who did had to work harder. We wanted the project to succeed.

_____

_____

4. Sue rode the train to work. There was a cow on the tracks. The train had to stop. Sue was five minutes late. _____

_____

5. Brad tried out for the football team. He weighs only eighty pounds. The coach told him to think about playing soccer. _____

_____

20.2 Sentence Combining • Practice 2

▶ **Exercise 1**   **Sentence Combining.**   Combine the sentences in each item, using a variety of methods.

EXAMPLE: The doctor examined Robert. He made a diagnosis.

_____ *After examining Robert, the doctor made a diagnosis.* _____

1. Joan stood outside the door. Another girl was with her.

    _____

2. Our play director was late. Several players were late too.

    _____

3. All contestants must answer difficult questions. College professors have prepared these questions.

    _____

4. The fish explored the sunken tire. They swam in and out.

    _____

5. William Hicks is Clayburgh's mayor. He will speak at tomorrow's dedication ceremony.

    _____

6. Many new books have been written about the future. This is a very popular subject.

    _____

7. Berlin was once divided into two parts. So was the rest of Germany.

    _____

8. Elizabeth dropped the toast. She was shocked.

    _____

9. Henry Clay never became President. He was a Westerner.

    _____

10. Holidays seldom fall in the summer. Spring also has few.

    _____

▶ **Exercise 2**   **Combining Sentences in a Passage.**   Rewrite the following passage, combining some of the sentences.

   (1) Danny heard the clumping of the boots on the upper deck. (2) He knew the pirates would walk in. (3) They would find him. (4) He hid in a barrel. (5) Captain Block and three of his men entered. (6) They dropped a heavy bundle onto a table. (7) Danny could hear this. (8) He strained his ears to overhear their conversation. (9) The pirates spoke in low tones. (10) Could they be looking for him?

_____

_____

_____

_____

_____

_____

_____

_____

20.3 Vary Sentence Openings and Structures
• Practice 1

Using Different Sentence Openers and Structures   Use a variety of sentence openers and structures in your writing.

SENTENCE OPENERS
Modifier First: Regretfully, Herman accepted the diamond ring back. Phrase First: After being lost for hours, we were glad to see camp again. Clause First: Although the car needed some work, the price was right.

Monotonous Sentences	Varied Sentences
Early warning of fire is important. It can be the key to a safe escape. Many people believe they will wake up if their house fills with smoke. This is not the case too often. Smoke detectors will sound a warning. They are quite inexpensive. There will still be time to get out.	Early warning can be the key to a safe escape from fire. Although many people believe they will wake up if their house or apartment fills with smoke, too often this is not the case. Smoke detectors, which are quite inexpensive, will sound a warning while there is still time to get out.

▶ **Exercise 1**   **Using Different Sentence Openers.**   Rewrite each sentence to make it begin with a one-word modifier, a phrase, or a clause.

EXAMPLE: The twins eyed their sister's new bicycle enviously.

Enviously, the twins eyed their sister's new bicycle.

1. Consult your Yellow Pages for the Willis Widget Store nearest you.

   _____

2. Some large cities in America have gone back to streetcars in recent years.

   _____

3. The elevator will not operate unless the door is closed.

   _____

4. Cheering fans swarmed onto the field after the game.

   _____

5. The President accepted the secretary's resignation reluctantly.

   _____

▶ **Exercise 2**   **Using Different Sentence Structures.**   Rewrite the following paragraph, using a variety of sentence structures. You may combine sentences or rearrange ideas.

(1) A fire extinguisher is a device for putting out fires. (2) Hardware stores stock several different kinds. (3) These kinds differ as to the flammable material on which they can be used. (4) The kind of fires an extinguisher will put out are listed on the nameplate. (5) The nameplate is attached to the front of the device. (6) Home fire extinguishers are useful. (7) But they do have a short discharge time. (8) This lasts from 8 to 24 seconds. (9) The uses must be accurate. (10) The user must direct the spray at the base of the fire.

_____

_____

_____

_____

_____

_____

20.3 Vary Sentence Openings and Structures
• Practice 2

▶ **Exercise 1** **Choosing Different Sentence Openers.** Rewrite each sentence so that no sentence begins with a subject.

EXAMPLE: The people avoided the ravine for some reason.
> *For some reason the people avoided the ravine.*

1. Mourners marched solemnly along the beach.

_____

2. We could not get the car started until Geoffrey arrived.

_____

3. He was seething with anger and waved his fist at us.

_____

4. R. F. Travers was a concert pianist who traveled the college circuit and performed for free.

_____

5. No one, however, could determine why the mixture changed color when it was heated.

_____

6. A thousand acorns tumbled down the attic stairs.

_____

7. You must assemble the right brushes, paints, and canvas to begin painting.

_____

8. Too many lives were lost sadly enough because lifesaving precautions had not been taken.

_____

9. Our food was cold by the time we returned from league practice.

_____

10. A hooded figure standing at the foot of the stairs blocked any chance of escape.

_____

▶ **Exercise 2** **Using Different Sentence Structures.** Rewrite the following passage, using a variety of sentence structures.

(1) I was on my own for about an hour, so I walked along the beach. (2) I began my walk near a huge, square-shaped rock, and I stopped periodically to study unusual pebbles and shells in the sand. (3) At that moment they seemed so unique and marvelous, but they might seem drab and dull at other times.

(4) I lost interest soon in the collection of pebbles and shells. (5) They were all along the beach. (6) I moved on. (7) Further on the sand was almost pure white. (8) Nothing littered the beach. (9) I could not hold myself back finally. (10) I took a running start and I ran splashing into the water.

_____

_____

_____

_____

_____

_____

_____

_____

_____

20.3 Vary Sentence Patterns • Practice 1

Using Different Sentence Patterns   Use similar patterns within sentences and groups of sentences to underscore ideas. Use a new structure after a series of similar ones to draw attention to contrast or to a final idea.

USING STRUCTURAL SIMILARITIES	
Within a Sentence	**Within a Group of Sentences**
Going for coffee and sandwiches, inking in changes in the scripts, making hairdressers' appointments for the stars, and *walking the director's dog* were not the activities Wendy had envisioned in her dreams of Broadway.	The expression "dollar to death" used by garage mechanics is an apt one. *Your car's alternator fails. That's not too expensive. Next the brake cylinders must be replaced. That's not too bad, either.* Gradually, you learn that many minor repairs mount up to a ruinous total.

USING STRUCTURAL DIFFERENCES
The usual programming on television was replaced by continuous newscasts presided over by sober newspeople. Beethoven's Funeral March alternated with Chopin's. Silent crowds gathered around the large billboards that had been erected in the squares. *The king was dead.*

▶ **Exercise 1**   **Using Structural Similarities Within Sentences.**   Choose three of the following topics or make up topics of your own. For each topic you choose, write a sentence in which you use parallel words, phrases, or clauses to emphasize your idea.

EXAMPLE: mountain climbing

> *The idea of climbing sheer rock faces, braving frigid winds, and dangling from ropes did not greatly appeal to Allen.*

a fireworks display	searching for a lost sneaker	how to start a car
a busy air terminal	arguments for or against censorship	training a dog

1. _____

2. _____

3. _____

▶ **Exercise 2**   **Using Structural Similarities Within Groups of Sentences.**   Choose two of the following topics. For each topic, write a brief passage of four or more sentences covering the items listed and any others you may wish to add. In the first passage, use similar sentence structures to call attention to the relationships among details. In the second passage, set up a pattern of sentence structures and then break the pattern.

1. Safety measures to avoid fires in the home: keeping matches away from children; cleaning out attics and cellars; storing flammable materials outside the home; checking electrical systems for defects

2. Ways to prevent home accidents; good lighting in halls and stairways; keeping halls and passageways clear; removing articles from steps and stairways

3. Things a babysitter should know: when children should go to bed; any special health problems; rules about snacks, TVs, and radio; whom to call in an emergency

_____

_____

_____

_____

_____

_____

20.3 Vary Sentence Patterns • Practice 2

▶ **Exercise 1** **Using Structural Similarities Within Sentences.** Choose one of the following topics as a basis for a sentence in which you use parallel words, phrases, or clauses to emphasize an idea and create a pattern.

An old cemetery	A scary movie
A difficult task	A bus ride
A pier with ships	A special phone call
An insect	A friend's house

_____

_____

_____

_____

▶ **Exercise 2** **Using Structural Similarities Within Groups of Sentences.** Choose one of the following topics and write a brief passage of four or more sentences. Use similar sentence structures to call attention to the relationship among the details.

1. Reasons why a building was condemned: faulty wiring, crumbling steps, a rusted and broken fire escape, falling roof and ceilings

2. Safety measures instituted by the school principal: running in hallways forbidden, weekly fire drills, volunteer student hall monitors, and washroom attendants

3. Reasons why Thorpe's Diner closed: could not keep good waiters and waitresses, had an inexperienced cook, lost business when a new freeway rerouted traffic

4. Things that a potential homeowner should look for: cracks in the foundation, leaks or sagging timbers in the roof, evidence of fire damage, improperly fitted pipes

5. Elements of a suspense story: mysterious characters, an unusual setting, unexplained events or unsolved crimes

_____

_____

_____

_____

_____

_____

▶ **Exercise 3** **Using Structural Differences.** Choose another topic from Exercise 2 and write another passage of four or more sentences. In this passage, set up a pattern and then break it to bring the passage to a strong, satisfying end.

_____

_____

_____

_____

_____

_____

Name _____ Date _____

 20.3 # Vary Sentence Length • Practice 1

Expanding Short Sentences   Expand short, choppy sentences by adding details.

Short Sentences	Expanded Sentences
The man walked down the street. They waved banners and signs.	The aging man walked down the empty dead-end street. They waved their colored banners and handmade signs to spur the team on to victory.

Shortening Long Sentences   Simplify rambling sentences either by separating them into simpler sentences or by moving and regrouping ideas.

Long, Rambling Sentences	Simpler, Clearer Sentences
Lois tried for weeks to find a part-time job after school and on weekends to earn money for her college expenses, and she finally settled for a job as a mother's helper but had hoped to find something related to her interest in economics.	To earn money for college expenses, Lois tried for weeks to find an after-school and weekend job. Although she had hoped for something related to her interest in economics, she finally settled for a job as a mother's helper.

▶ **Exercise 1**   **Expanding Short Sentences.**   Improve each of the sentences by adding details.

EXAMPLE: Candy studied for her test.

_____ *Candy spent several hours studying for her English test.* _____

1. John flew across the country.

   _____

2. Liz was trapped inside the cabin.

   _____

3. The police arrested Orville Jones.

   _____

4. A man waited outside the house.

   _____

▶ **Exercise 2**   **Simplifying Long Sentences.**   Rewrite each sentence as two more simpler, clearer sentences. If necessary, refer to the model in the second chart above.

1. The family reunion and barbeque is an annual tradition and it is hosted by a different branch of the family each year, so when our turn came we decided to hold it at Jackson Park because it has a convenient location and excellent facilities.

   _____

   _____

   _____

2. Rescuers worked all through the night as they pulled pieces of wreckage from the water and searched for survivors, and at dawn they redoubled their efforts but the search was fruitless.

   _____

   _____

   _____

20.3 Vary Sentence Length • Practice 2

▷ **Exercise 1** **Adding Details.** Expand each short sentence by adding details.

EXAMPLE: The sprinter crossed the finish line.

Gasping for air, the sprinter crossed the finish line a stride ahead of his rival.

1. The rain fell. _____

_____

2. The train passed us. _____

_____

3. I looked at the sunrise. _____

_____

4. The dog smelled bacon. _____

_____

5. The tugboat helped the ocean liner turn around. _____

_____

6. My grades were falling. _____

_____

7. Harold had to work on Thanksgiving. _____

_____

8. Rumors circulated during lunch. _____

_____

9. The fire destroyed many square miles of forest. _____

_____

10. It was a good movie. _____

_____

▷ **Exercise 2** **Simplifying Long Sentences.** Rewrite the following paragraph, separating and regrouping ideas.

(1) A long bus ride down an interstate highway, more than a trip on a train or plane, encourages deep thoughts, unless you are a person who is addicted to reading, because there are fewer distractions that take your concentration away from the ideas that are unfolding in your mind. (2) Since there are no people walking up and down the aisle, there is no food being served, there is no movie to watch, there are no traffic lights or highway signs to watch for, and, except for certain parts of the country, the scenery along the interstates is usually monotonous, you can daydream and plan.

_____

_____

_____

_____

_____

_____

_____

20.4 # Fragments • **Practice 1**

Fragments   A fragment is a group of words that does not express a complete thought. Do not confuse a phrase, a series, or a subordinate clause with a complete sentence.

Fragments	Complete Sentences
At the end of a long path,	There is a hut *at the end of the long path.*
Walking in circles.	The girl, *walking in circles,* asked for help.
A pen, some notes, and a dictionary.	To the library she brought *a pen, some notes, and a dictionary.*
If you want my advice.	*If you want my advice,* tell your mother.
Which she described to me.	The dress, *which she described to me,* has been sold.

▶ **Exercise 1**   **Distinguishing Between Fragments and Complete Sentences.**   Write whether each group of words is a sentence or a fragment.

EXAMPLE: Near the road not far from the hill.   _____*fragment*_____

1. Since your appointment is later in the day. _____

2. She enjoys waffles and ice cream. _____

3. Two pounds of apples and a bag of potatoes. _____

4. What you asked me yesterday. _____

5. In the morning the police called. _____

6. In the back room of the library. _____

7. Because we wanted it very much. _____

8. My friends, my family, and my teachers. _____

9. This is the absolute truth. _____

10. Whom you asked me about. _____

▶ **Exercise 2**   **Changing Fragments into Complete Sentences.**   Each item below is a fragment. Add whatever is necessary to make it into a complete sentence.

EXAMPLE: Reaching the police.   _____*Reaching the police, we reported the accident.*_____

1. In back of the book. _____

2. Feeling sad. _____

3. When she called. _____

4. Bread, milk, and soap. _____

5. Which you offered. _____

6. If you can come. _____

7. Walking in the park. _____

8. Near us. _____

9. As they expected. _____

10. Along the road very close to the bridge. _____

20.4 Fragments • Practice 2

▶ **Exercise 1** **Identifying and Correcting Fragments.** If the words in a numbered item form one or more complete sentences, write correct. If the item contains a fragment, rewrite it to make it a complete sentence.

EXAMPLE: The doctor was late. With whom I had an appointment.

_____*The doctor with whom I had an appointment was late.*_____

1. I finally found the missing book. A collection of quotations from famous contemporary politicians.

_____

_____

2. Dozens of young athletes gathered for the final meet. _____

_____

3. Sipped at the steaming cup of coffee. _____

_____

4. The young boy impressed by the sight of the men marching off to war. _____

_____

5. The window had been smashed with a crowbar. At the rear of the car. _____

_____

6. The apartment manager gave the tenants their notice. They had thirty days to vacate. _____

_____

7. It was only much later that the couple learned. Who the pickpocket was. _____

_____

8. The willow trees with their branches bending gracefully low, the lush green grass, and the waves of the lake gently lapping the shore. _____

_____

9. The footsteps echoing down the long, deserted corridor. _____

_____

10. I needed another quarter for the washing machine. _____

_____

▶ **Exercise 2** **Correcting Fragments.** The following paragraphs contain five fragments. Rewrite each fragment to make it a complete sentence.

EXAMPLE: Walking along the jetty. _____*As I was walking along the jetty, I saw a schooner on the bay.*_____

Frustration seems to be a normal part of life. Most people learn about frustration. At a very early age. Children can be observed bursting into tears. As they try again and again to tie their shoelaces. Grown men and women often lose their tempers playing golf. When they make a poor shot.

It is not unusual. To have trouble learning something new. No matter how hard you try sometimes, you just can't do something well. It happens at school. At work and when playing games.

1. _____

2. _____

3. _____

4. _____

5. _____

20.4 Run-ons • Practice 1

Run-on Sentences A run-on sentence consists of two or more complete sentences that are not properly joined or punctuated. Some run-ons have a comma separating two independent clauses. This is not enough. To correct a run-on sentence, use a comma and a coordinating conjunction, a semicolon, an end mark, or a new sentence structure.

Run-on Sentences	Properly Punctuated Sentences
She asked me to go, I agreed.	She asked me to go, and I agreed. (comma and coordinating conjunction)
We made an offer they rejected it.	We made an offer; they rejected it. (punctuated with a semicolon)
I can't explain my feelings, I just want to be left alone.	I can't explain my feelings. I just want to be left alone. (changed into two sentences)

▶ **Exercise 1** **Distinguishing Between Run-ons and Properly Punctuated Sentences.** If the sentence is a run-on, write *RO*. If the sentence is correct, write *S*.

EXAMPLE: I smiled, she turned her head. ___*RO*___

1. Mrs. Rand spoke softly I listened carefully. _____

2. I know the answer, I won't tell it to you. _____

3. Mary offered to help them get to the station. _____

4. We opened the box it contained business envelopes. _____

5. There has been a change of plans. _____

6. The trains are quicker the buses are less expensive. _____

7. I understand the problem, she doesn't. _____

8. This is my reply I won't change my mind. _____

9. We need aspirins for the house I need shaving cream. _____

10. Rochester and Buffalo are important cities; Albany, however, is the capital of New York. _____

▶ **Exercise 2** **Changing Run-ons into Properly Punctuated Sentences.** Correct each run-on.

EXAMPLE: I waved, she nodded back. ___*I waved, and she nodded back.*___

1. Is this your answer I can't believe it.

    _____

2. Here are three recipes, tell me which one you like best.

    _____

3. My cousin collects baseball cards I collect coins.

    _____

4. We saw the accident, clearly, nobody was really at fault.

    _____

5. The President issued a short statement, his press secretary filled in the details.

    _____

20.4 Run-ons • Practice 2

▶ **Exercise 1**   **Identifying and Correcting Run-on Sentences.**   If a sentence is correct as written, write *correct*. If it is a run-on, rewrite it to make it correct. Use each of the four methods of correcting run-ons at least once.

1. I play the piano for many musicals moreover I give lessons to twenty students. _____
_____

2. The electricity went out I searched for the candles. _____

3. I lost the first chess game, but I won the second. _____

4. As a boy, my dad could go to the movies for seventy-five cents, it cost thirty-five cents for the movie and forty cents for the popcorn and a drink. _____
_____

5. The roads were crowded with families leaving for the three-day weekend. _____
_____

6. What time is the party, will you pick me up? _____

7. The first raindrops fell we raced for cover. _____

8. Adult education classes will be taught this semester, the school will not offer a class in Chinese cooking. _____
_____

9. I called to him however he had already driven away. _____
_____

10. We earned money washing cars, therefore, we could afford to go to the concert. _____
_____

▶ **Writing Application**   **Locating and Correcting Fragments and Run-ons.**   If a numbered item contains an error, rewrite it to make it correct. If it does not contain an error, write *correct*.

1. The Census Bureau counts the American people. Once every ten years. _____
_____

2. Each decade, every man, woman, and child is counted, tabulated, and translated into statistics, they tell us the average income of Americans, the percentage of female graduates, the typical life span, and many other vital pieces of information. _____
_____

3. Important decisions resulted from these census profiles. Apportionment for the federal legislature, as well as distribution of sought-after federal funds. _____
_____

4. Some advertising companies even develop marketing strategies after studying the trends. Then graph predictions for the next ten-year span. _____
_____

5. Who does all this counting? The Census Bureau with over two thousand professionals and 275,000 temporary census takers. _____
_____

20.5 # Misplaced Modifiers • **Practice 1**

Misplaced Modifiers   A misplaced modifier seems to modify the wrong word in the sentence. It should be placed as close as possible to the word it modifies.

MISPLACED MODIFIERS	
Misplaced	**Improved**
We bought an album at that store *that cost three dollars.*	At the store we bought an album *that cost three dollars.*
The thief missed the necklace on the bed *in a box.*	The thief missed the necklace *in a box* on the bed.

▷ **Exercise 1**   **Recognizing Misplaced Modifiers.**   Underline each misplaced modifier. If the sentence is correct, leave it unmarked.

EXAMPLE: The musician signed autographs <u>with a clarinet in hand.</u>

1. The house was broken into that he recently purchased.

2. Bob gave his cassette deck to his sister with Dolby.

3. The book won a prize with many color photos.

4. Damaged in the accident, Phil saw his car in the repair shop.

5. The books that you want will cost thirty-five dollars.

6. The man asked to see the surgeon growing restless in the hospital.

7. The bus is leaving for the city with your luggage in it.

8. The mirror reflected the view in the silver frame.

9. The room with a view of the sea has been rented.

10. We saw many art galleries driving from city to city.

▷ **Exercise 2**   **Correcting Misplaced Modifiers.**   Rewrite the sentences below, improving the position of the misplaced modifiers.

EXAMPLE: The only store is closed in town.

<u>*The only store in town is closed.*</u>

1. We need two more things from the store to eat for lunch.

_____

2. The car hit a spectator leading the parade.

_____

3. Bruce ordered a soda and a sandwich with chocolate ice cream.

_____

4. My sisters ran from the gazebo shouting my name.

_____

5. John reminded me to remember my notebook twice.

_____

20.5 Misplaced Modifiers • Practice 2

▶ **Exercise 1** **Identifying and Correcting Misplaced Modifiers.** Write each sentence, correcting all misplaced modifiers.

1. The pianist played a new composition sitting on the piano bench. _____

_____

2. Turning green, I watched the lights. _____

3. We boarded the train with three suitcases heading toward our winter home in Florida. _____

_____

4. We heard the bus had crashed on the radio. _____

_____

5. I arranged the flowers for my mother using the new vase. _____

_____

6. Cranky and tired, I put the baby down for a nap. _____

_____

7. The seals looked hopefully at us desiring more sardines. _____

_____

8. Growling with hunger, I listened to my empty stomach. _____

_____

9. We heard that a forest fire had started nearby while preparing to go on vacation. _____

_____

10. Barking loudly at the squirrel, I frowned at the dog. _____

_____

▶ **Exercise 2** **Identifying and Correcting Misplaced Modifiers.** The following paragraphs contain ten misplaced modifiers. Rewrite each sentence in which there is a misplaced modifier so that the position of the modifier is improved.

Sagging and needing repair, Mrs. Henderson called the construction company to fix her porch. Too busy to come out immediately, she had to wait two weeks. Staring at the damage, an idea began to form in her mind. When in high school, shop had been one of her classes she thought, optimistically, that the porch might be easy enough to fix herself.

Getting out her tools, the excitement began to build. After working for several days, the porch was disassembled. Finding the problem, the supports had to be replaced. Going to the lumber store, the wood was not very expensive. Piling the wood into the truck, the back window was blocked. Driving home, the mirrors on the sides of the truck were very useful.

1. _____
2. _____
3. _____
4. _____
5. _____
6. _____
7. _____
8. _____
9. _____
10. _____

Name _____ Date _____

 20.5 # Dangling Modifiers • Practice 1

Dangling Modifiers A dangling modifier seems to modify the wrong word or no word at all because the word it should modify has been omitted from the sentence.

DANGLING MODIFIERS	
Dangling	**Improved**
Walking to school, her notebook was lost.	Walking to school, she lost her notebook.
When she was still in grade school, Alice's aunt bought a house in Kansas.	*When Alice was still in grade school*, her aunt bought a house in Kansas.

▶ **Exercise 1** **Recognizing Dangling Modifiers.** Underline each dangling modifier. If a sentence has no dangling modifier, leave it unmarked.

EXAMPLE: There were two meal stops <u>driving to Atlanta</u>.

 1. Eating in the restaurant, his manners were deplorable.
 2. Brought before the judge, the plea was not guilty.
 3. Snatched from its mother's arms, the child cried pitifully.
 4. Performing before a real audience, her talent was quickly recognized.
 5. Swimming in the pool, his chores were left undone.
 6. A group of new houses were needed entering the development.
 7. Turning the corner, I saw my mother and father.
 8. To bake a cake, all the ingredients should be assembled first.
 9. Driving from the hotel, the Rideau Canal was seen on the left.
10. After I opened the letter, I realized my good fortune.

▶ **Exercise 2** **More Work with Dangling Modifiers.** Underline each dangling modifier. If a sentence has no dangling modifier, leave it unmarked.

EXAMPLE: <u>Frightened by the announcement</u>, the room was silent.

 1. When he was a cadet at West Point, John's father became a four-star general.
 2. Running rather slowly, the library seemed a distant goal.
 3. While practicing in the gym, sneakers must always be worn.
 4. Sinking rapidly, the pool was soon empty.
 5. Many different kinds of barns were seen cruising along the country road.
 6. When Audrey appeared at the door, I shouted for joy.
 7. Looking at the catalog, an expensive lamp stood out.
 8. Sweeping up Lexington Avenue, his long beard was the center of attention.
 9. Trampling through the snow, her bags began to tear.
10. Her towel could not be found leaving the shower.

© Prentice-Hall, Inc.   Dangling Modifiers • 77

20.5 Dangling Modifiers • Practice 2

▶ **Exercise 1** **Identifying and Correcting Dangling Modifiers.** If a sentence is correct, write *correct*. If a sentence contains a dangling modifier, correct it.

EXAMPLE: To compete in the race, a form must be completed.
        To compete in the race, you must complete a form.

1. Wrapped in my blanket, the cold was no problem. _____

_____

2. To knit a sweater, all the yarn must be bought at once. _____

_____

3. Having ignored the problem, little could now be done. _____

_____

4. To get the job, my references must be verified. _____

_____

5. While taking inventory, the store was closed. _____

_____

6. When he was a baby, John's father was elected mayor. _____

_____

7. After examining the evidence, the defendant was released. _____

_____

8. When the cat scratched at the door, we let her in. _____

_____

9. Cutting out all the wordiness, the essay was improved. _____

_____

10. When not talking, the room was filled with laughter. _____

_____

▶ **Writing Application** **Avoiding Misplaced and Dangling Modifiers.** Make each item into a complete sentence, using the construction in parentheses. Make sure that you do not use any misplaced or dangling modifiers.

EXAMPLE: While doing my homework, (independent clause).
        While doing my homework, I was interrupted three times.

1. After working hard all day, (independent clause).

_____

2. (infinitive phrase), I needed a large down payment.

_____

3. (participial phrase), Roger caught sight of a large fish.

_____

4. We watched the survivors rescued (prepositional phrase).

_____

5. After (gerund phrase), I could not stop choking.

_____

20.6 Using Parallelism • Practice 1

Recognizing the Correct Use of Parallelism   Parallelism is the placement of equal ideas in words, phrases, or clauses of similar types.

PARALLEL WORDS, PHRASES, AND CLAUSES
Words: We *hiked, swam,* and *rested* on our vacation.
Phrases: My sisters shopped *in the mall* and *in some local shops.*
Clauses: I wondered *who discovered the valley* and *who built the first settlements there.*

▶ **Exercise 1**   **Recognizing Parallel Structures.**   In each sentence below, underline the parallel structures.

EXAMPLE: She went <u>to school</u>, <u>to the library</u>, and <u>to work</u>.

1. In the mall she bought boots, stockings, and gloves.
2. There are many unusual species in the forest and in the dry areas.
3. Growing up alone and learning to be independent, Pat succeeded early in life.
4. In a burst of emotion the actor smiled, snarled, grimaced, and whimpered.
5. She knew that one of the boys liked country music and that the other liked hard rock.
6. Ricky studies on the bus, at school, and at work.
7. The twins were busy wrapping packages and tying ribbons.
8. Twisting and turning, he managed to wriggle from the handcuffs.
9. He decided to wash his car, to repair the fender, and to change the oil.
10. Nancy, Betty, and I all agreed to work overtime.

▶ **Exercise 2**   **Completing Parallel Structures.**   In the spaces provided, add an appropriate parallel structure.

EXAMPLE: I read the passage, thought about it, and ____*decided to act*____ .

1. The room was dark, dreary, and _____.
2. We decided to go uptown, to have lunch, and _____.
3. Sally, Ellen, and _____.
4. When you arrived late and when _____, I fully understood your predicament.
5. I will write a good speech, rehearse it carefully, and _____

   _____
6. The orchestra played an overture, a march, and a _____.
7. I will buy the ingredients, bake the cookies, and _____.
8. Smiling and _____, Tim accepted the award.
9. Roads are jammed at the bridge and _____.
10. I need two blouses, several skirts, and _____.

20.6 Using Parallelism • Practice 2

Exercise 1 Recognizing Parallel Structures. Underline the parallel structures in each sentence. Then identify what each is composed of: *words*, *phrases*, or *clauses*.

EXAMPLE: Swimming during the summer, skiing during the winter, and running daily keep me fit.

_____*phrases*_____

1. In our garden, we planted tomatoes, squash, and lettuce. _____

2. My evenings are spent doing homework, watching television, or crocheting an afghan. _____

3. The rain fell steadily; the wind howled mournfully. _____

4. All of the puppies gleefully hopped, jumped, and cavorted. _____

5. We looked at slides that showed us opening presents, blowing out candles, and eating ice cream and cake. _____

6. The road was deserted, rain was falling, and we were lost. _____

7. He ran out the door, down the steps, and across the street. _____

8. On vacation I wore sweaters, jeans, and sneakers every day. _____

9. Success is what I hope for, what I work hard for, and what I deserve. _____

10. Walking the dog and cleaning my room are two of my chores. _____

Exercise 2 Writing Parallel Structures in Sentences. Complete each of the following sentences by writing additional parallel elements in the blanks. Then underline the kind of parallel elements you wrote.

EXAMPLE: I like to run, ____*dance*____, ____*sing*____, and ____*swim*____. (words, phrases, clauses)

1. I study before school, _____, and _____. (words, phrases, clauses)

2. James recommended the movie because it was interesting, _____, _____, and _____. (words, phrases, clauses)

3. Pam's party will be on Saturday, _____, _____, _____. (words, phrases, clauses)

4. I will help if you need me, _____, and _____.(words, phrases, clauses)

5. His advice was to take two aspirins, _____, and _____. (words, phrases, clauses)

6. If I could afford it, I would buy a new coat, _____, _____, and _____. (words, phrases, clauses)

7. Marylou put carrots, _____, _____, and _____ into the soup. (words, phrases, clauses)

8. All the aunts, _____, _____, and _____ came to the reunion. (words, phrases, clauses)

9. We drove over the hill, _____, and _____ to get to Grandma's house. (words, phrases, clauses)

10. When you dance, _____, and _____, you really seem to enjoy yourself. (words, phrases, clauses)

20.6 Faulty Parallelism • Practice 1

Correcting Faulty Parallelism   Correct a sentence containing faulty parallelism by rewriting it so that each parallel idea is expressed in the same grammatical structure. Faulty parallelism can involve words, phrases, and clauses in a series as well as comparisons.

CORRECTING FAULTY PARALLELISM
GERUND PHRASE   GERUND PHRASE   INFINITIVE PHRASE Incorrect: I enjoy *reading books, listening to music,* and *to collect stamps.*
GERUND PHRASE   GERUND PHRASE   GERUND PHRASE Correct: I enjoy *reading books, listening to music,* and *collecting stamps.*
NOUN   GERUND PHRASE Incorrect: She prefers a good *meal* to *going on a long hike.*
NOUN   NOUN Correct: She prefers a good *meal* to a long *hike.*

▶ **Exercise 1**   **Recognizing Faulty Parallelism.**   Next to each sentence below write *FP* if there is faulty parallelism and *C* if it is correct.

EXAMPLE: I want to sing, to dance, and acting. _____*FP*_____

1. I would rather visit a new city than going to a hotel. _____

2. She knows how to plan, how to take notes, and using a number of different references. _____

3. The roads are crowded in the morning and in the evening. _____

4. Ted likes jogging, dancing, and to go on hikes. _____

5. I want this car for its styling not that it was a good price. _____

6. My parents prefer visiting new places and to travel to foreign countries. _____

7. Our candidate is intelligent, compassionate, and trustworthy. _____

8. My grandmother likes to bake, to sew, and watching television. _____

9. Rest, exercise, and to eat good food are recommended. _____

10. I expect to visit London, to see Stonehenge, and to stay in Stratford. _____

▶ **Exercise 2**   **Writing Sentences with Parallel Structures.**   Follow the instructions below to write five sentences of your own.

1. Write a sentence with three verbs in a series.

_____

2. Combine two parallel clauses using *but.*

_____

3. Use three parallel predicate adjectives after a verb.

_____

4. Begin a sentence with two prepositional phrases connected by *and.*

_____

5. Use *and* to join two gerund phrases.

_____

_____

20.6 Faulty Parallelism • Practice 2

▶ **Exercise 1** **Correcting Faulty Parallelism.** Rewrite the sentences, putting each in proper parallel form.

EXAMPLE: She left me angry, frustrated, and wearing a frown.

_____ *She left me angry, frustrated, and frowning.* _____

1. We have things to do, people to see, and places that should be visited.

_____

2. I enjoy my job because of the opportunities it offers, the fringe benefits I receive, and I earn a good salary.

_____

3. We should invite people with whom you work and your friends from the swim club.

_____

4. I have poor handwriting more because I am careless than that I have never been taught.

_____

5. If I have the money and time becomes available, I will go.

_____

6. The couple did not like the house since it had poor plumbing, and they would need to landscape the yard.

_____

7. The comedian was clever, original, and kept us laughing.

_____

8. I had steak, Tanya ate flounder, but a hamburger is all that Steve ordered.

_____

9. I voted for the sale of state bonds, for more state parks, and to have the state cut property taxes.

_____

10. My father both prepared the main course and the dessert.

_____

▶ **Writing Application** **Writing Sentences Containing Parallel Structures.** Use the following instructions to write ten sentences, each containing a parallel construction.

1. Write a sentence containing a series of three adjectives.

_____

2. Write a sentence containing three parallel words.

_____

3. Use *and* to join two gerund phrases.

_____

4. Construct a sentence with a series of three prepositional phrases.

_____

5. Use *either . . . or* to join two infinitive phrases.

_____

20.7 # Recognizing Faulty Coordination • **Practice 1**

Recognizing Faulty Coordination Use *and* or other coordinating conjunctions only to connect related ideas of equal importance.

FAULTY COORDINATION
Miss Grant is an expert on Indian artifacts, *and* she likes very rich desserts. Few writers can compare with Mark Twain, *and* I always liked *Huckleberry Finn*. He wants to have a garden, *and* our tomatoes are ripe.

▶ **Exercise 1** **Recognizing Faulty Coordination.** For the five sentences below in which coordination is used correctly, write *correct.* For the others, write *faulty.*

EXAMPLE: Chrysler has a reputation for well-built cars, and I bought a used Dodge Dart. ___*faulty*___

1. My father always enjoyed fishing, and he fought hard in the war. _____

2. Charles Dickens was one of England's most respected writers, and he made a highly publicized trip to America. _____

3. Bill drove to the meeting in Philadelphia, and the rest of the staff flew down. _____

4. Harvard was founded in 1633, and Yale was founded in 1701. _____

5. Grandma's chocolate chip cookies are the best, and she gets terrible migraine headaches. _____

6. The house is not yet finished, and the couple hopes to have a large family some day. _____

7. My first thought was of you, and my second was of Harry. _____

8. Marie took a deep breath, and her diving equipment had not been carefully checked. _____

9. Nathaniel Gorham and Rufus King signed the Constitution for Massachusetts, and John Langdom and Nicholas Gilman signed it for New Hampshire. _____

10. The trains are right on schedule, and the buses are also on time today. _____

▶ **Exercise 2** **Using Coordination Correctly.** Write five compound sentences, using *and* correctly.

EXAMPLE: ___*I like fishing, and I also like fish fries.*___

1. _____

2. _____

3. _____

4. _____

5. _____

20.7 Recognizing Faulty Coordination • Practice 2

▶ **Exercise 1**   **Identifying Correct and Faulty Coordination.**   For the five sentences in which coordination is used correctly, write *correct*. For the others, write *faulty*.

EXAMPLE: I made the dessert, and it was an apple pie. ___*faulty*___

1. The dry ingredients have been mixed, and the eggs have been thoroughly

   beaten. _____

2. A storm at sea can be frightening, and our boat was called *Daisy*. _____

3. Samuel Clemens is a famous American writer, and he used the pen name Mark

   Twain. _____

4. I will slim down for the swim meet, and I will then swim much faster. _____

5. The artist finished the layouts, and the leaflets were taken to the printers. _____

6. My tires need to be realigned, and the brakes need to be adjusted. _____

7. The construction company finished the building, and the supplies arrived, and we stocked the

   shelves, but our clerks needed training, and that will take several weeks. _____

8. It was the grand opening of the restaurant, and hundreds of people were waiting to

   enter. _____

9. At the nearby shopping center is a small restaurant, and it boasts that it has the best homemade pies

   in town. _____

10. The actor's newest movie was just released, but it is a science fiction

    picture. _____

▶ **Exercise 2**   **Identifying Correct and Faulty Coordination.**   The following paragraphs contain five examples of faulty coordination. On the line, write each sentence that has faulty coordination.

   Gene had an examination the next day, and he got home late. He had gone to the library, and he had studied for several hours, and he was feeling very tired. The examination was going to be in biology, and Gene wasn't very good at biology. Even though he paid attention in class, he just couldn't remember everything. The scientific terms were confusing, difficult, and they were also hard to pronounce.

   Gene's father gave him some advice and he told him to review his notes once and get plenty of rest. "If you don't do well in biology, don't worry, son," said his father. "You can take it as a sign that it's just not your field. You know that you're good in English, Spanish, and history." This advice was music to Gene's ears.

   That night, he slept well. He was no longer worried about the test. His father's advice made a lot of sense, and Gene was not going to feel stress about the test, and it would be a fine day.

1. _____

2. _____

3. _____

4. _____

5. _____

20.7 Correcting Faulty Coordination • Practice 1

Correcting Faulty Coordination   Revise sentences with faulty coordination by putting unrelated ideas into separate sentences or by putting a less important or subordinate idea into a subordinate clause or phrase.

CORRECTING FAULTY COORDINATION
Faulty: James Joyce spent many years in exile abroad, and he wrote a collection of short stories called *Dubliners*.
Correct: James Joyce spent many years in exile abroad. He wrote a collection of short stories called *Dubliners*.
Faulty: Pat is afraid of honeybees, and they are necessary for cross-pollination.
Correct: Although Pat is afraid of honeybees, they are necessary for cross-pollination.

▶ **Exercise 1**   **Correcting Faulty Coordination.**   Correct the faulty coordination in the sentences below.

EXAMPLE: My favorite artist is Mary Cassatt, and she died in 1926.

　　　　My favorite artist is Mary Cassatt, who died in 1926.

1. The Carlsbad Caverns are in New Mexico, and we visited them last summer.

   _____

2. The children were ready at noon, and their parents arrived at three.

   _____

3. The stores were filled with shoppers, and the parking lot was not full.

   _____

4. Jennifer liked her new school, and she wrote a letter every week.

   _____

5. Albert Einstein was a brilliant scientist, and he left Germany before World War II.

   _____

▶ **Exercise 2**   **More Work with Faulty Coordination.**   Correct each of the following stringy sentences.

1. She was a friendly person, and she liked to meet new people, and she often took trips just to meet people. _____

   _____

2. Keith sprained his ankle skiing, and he was forced to spend the rest of the week in the lodge, and he played a lot of chess. _____

   _____

3. Wendy is a talented singer, and she plays the guitar, and people like to hear her perform. _____

   _____

4. Frank failed his math test, and he was late for school, and he has been suspended for a week. _____

   _____

5. Irma was sunburned after a morning on the beach, and it was quite painful, and she decided to spend the afternoon inside. _____

   _____

20.7 Correcting Faulty Coordination • Practice 2

▶ **Exercise 1** **Correcting Faulty Coordination.** . Write each sentence, correcting the faulty coordination.

EXAMPLE: I made the dessert, and it was an apple pie.

_____I made the dessert, an apple pie._____

1. Clark Gable was one of America's most popular actors, and he starred in *Gone with the Wind*.

_____

2. I jogged to the park, and crowds filled the lawns.

_____

3. The lava flows stretch many miles in Hawaii, and they cut a swath through the otherwise dense vegetation.

_____

4. Someone built a miniature replica of the White House, and it has lights and a television that actually work.

_____

5. The suitcases were packed, and we set off on vacation.

_____

6. The alarm woke me up this morning, and it was still dark.

_____

7. Jill was looking for a job, and she had been fired last week.

_____

8. The clerk rang up my purchase, but she did it incorrectly, and I asked her to re-total it, and she did, but she made another mistake, and the manager finally fixed it.

_____

9. *Star Wars* was Tom's favorite movie, and he saw it eighteen times.

_____

10. The plan took off fifteen minutes behind schedule, and it arrived at its next stop on time.

_____

▶ **Writing Application** **Avoiding Faulty Coordination in Sentence Combining.** Combine each pair of sentences, avoiding faulty coordination.

EXAMPLE: Linda sings in the choir. She is a soprano. _____Linda, a soprano, sings in the choir.____

1. My eyelids felt heavy. I lay down for a rest on the couch.

_____

2. The clock chimed nine times. Bev knew she had overslept.

_____

3. Zip and Zoe, our dachshunds, play outside during the day. They sleep inside at night.

_____

4. The mountain climber was stranded by an unexpected blizzard. He had to be rescued by helicopter.

_____

5. Paul Zindel came to speak to us. He wrote *The Pigman*.

_____

21.1 Verb Tenses • Practice 1

The Six Verb Tenses   A tense is a form of a verb that shows the time of an action or state of being. There are six different tenses, each with a basic and progressive form. The present and past tenses also have an emphatic form.

Tenses	Basic Forms	Progressive Forms	Emphatic Forms
Present	I go	I am going	I do go
Past	I went	I was going	I did go
Future	I will go	I will be going	
Present Perfect	I have gone	I have been going	
Past Perfect	I had gone	I had been going	
Future Perfect	I will have gone	I will have been going	

The Four Principal Parts of Verbs   A verb has four principal parts: the present, the present participle, the past, and the past participle.

THE FOUR PRINCIPAL PARTS			
Present	Present Participle	Past	Past Participle
love	loving	loved	(have) loved
drive	driving	drove	(have) driven

▶ **Exercise 1**   **Recognizing Tenses and Forms of Verbs.**   Underline the verb or verb phrase in each sentence below. Then write the tense and form of the verb.

EXAMPLE: We <u>were</u> just <u>passing</u> by. _____*past progressive*_____

1. We take a bus in the mornings. _____
2. Paul will be going to a new school next fall. _____
3. The game ended a minute too soon. _____
4. I did wait on the corner. _____
5. It had been raining all day. _____
6. We have finally solved the puzzle. _____
7. The play will be over by them. _____
8. The team does play better at home. _____
9. I will return your book for you. _____
10. Jill is taking chemistry this year. _____

▶ **Exercise 2**   **Identifying Principal Parts.**   On the lines below, write the principal part used to form the verb in each sentence above. Then write the name of that principal part.

EXAMPLE: _____*passing, present participle*_____

1. _____   6. _____
2. _____   7. _____
3. _____   8. _____
4. _____   9. _____
5. _____   10. _____

21.1 Verb Tenses • Practice 2

▶ **Exercise 1**   **Recognizing Basic, Progressive, and Emphatic Forms.**   Identify the form of each verb as basic, progressive, or emphatic.

EXAMPLE: They have been dancing. _____*progressive*_____

1. I passed. _____

2. They have been studying. _____

3. It broke. _____

4. I do understand. _____

5. He was listening. _____

6. She was swimming. _____

7. He did forget. _____

8. We had lost. _____

9. They have left. _____

10. You will be driving. _____

▶ **Exercise 2**   **Recognizing the Six Tenses.**   Write the tense of each verb in Exercise 1. If the form is not basic, add the name of the form.

EXAMPLE: They have been dancing. _____*present perfect progressive*_____

1. _____	6. _____
2. _____	7. _____
3. _____	8. _____
4. _____	9. _____
5. _____	10. _____

▶ **Exercise 3**   **Recognizing Principal Parts.**   Identify the principal part used to form each verb in Exercise 1.

EXAMPLE: They have been dancing. _____*present participle*_____

1. _____	6. _____
2. _____	7. _____
3. _____	8. _____
4. _____	9. _____
5. _____	10. _____

© Prentice-Hall, Inc.

21.1 Regular and Irregular Verbs • Practice 1

Regular and Irregular Verbs   A regular verb is one whose past and past participle are formed by adding *-ed* or *-d* to the present form.

PRINCIPAL PARTS OF REGULAR VERBS			
Present	**Present Participle**	**Past**	**Past Participle**
form	forming	formed	(have) formed
like	liking	liked	(have) liked
stop	stopping	stopped	(have) stopped

An irregular verb is one whose past and past participle are not formed by adding *-ed* or *-d* to the present form.

PRINCIPAL PARTS OF REGULAR VERBS			
Present	**Present Participle**	**Past**	**Past Participle**
burst	bursting	burst	(have) burst
bring	bringing	brought	(have) brought
find	finding	found	(have) found
come	coming	came	(have) come
give	giving	went	(have) gone
shake	shaking	shook	(have) shaken

▶ **Exercise 1**   **Writing the Principal Parts of Irregular Verbs.**   Add the missing principal parts.

EXAMPLE: _sing_   _singing_   _sang_   _(have) sung_

1. _____ shrinking _____ _____
2. know _____ _____ _____
3. strike _____ _____ _____
4. _____ _____ went _____
5. _____ swimming _____ _____
6. _____ _____ _____ (have) paid
7. _____ breaking _____ _____
8. throw _____ _____ _____
9. _____ _____ _____ (have) drunk
10. _____ _____ rang _____

▶ **Exercise 2**   **Choosing the correct Form of Irregular Verbs.**   Fill in each blank with the correct verb form from those given in parentheses.

EXAMPLE: Bowser has ___eaten___ all the sandwiches.   (ate, eaten)

1. The wind has _____ a tree down in the park.   (blew, blown)
2. Food _____ less in those days than it does now.   (cost, costed)
3. The doctor has already _____ to the hospital.   (went, gone)
4. Yesterday, I _____ ten laps in the pool.   (swam, swum)
5. One more puff would have _____ that balloon.   (busted, burst)

21.1 Regular and Irregular Verbs • Practice 2

▶ **Exercise 1** **Learning the Principal Parts of Irregular Verbs.** Write the present participle, the past, and the past participle of each verb.

EXAMPLE: swim ___*swimming swam swum*___

1. keep _____
2. know _____
3. set _____
4. blow _____
5. lend _____

6. stride _____
7. fling _____
8. arise _____
9. lie _____
10. pay _____

▶ **Exercise 2** **Choosing the Correct Forms of Irregular Verbs.** Choose the correct form of the verb in parentheses.

EXAMPLE: I regretted I had (broke, broken) the antique. ___*broken*___

1. Anyone would have (ran, run) away in that situation. _____
2. After each success Barney (grew, growed) surer of himself. _____
3. The knight drew his sword and (slayed, slew) the dragon. _____
4. The team had (strove, striven) hard to win back the trophy. _____
5. Blake (shaken, shook) pepper over his food. _____
6. Mom and I (catched, caught) several beautiful butterflies. _____
7. He said he (saw, seen) some fine drawings by the children. _____
8. Mike (drawed, drew) a sketch of the history teacher. _____
9. The thief (creeped, crept) up the stairs. _____
10. Swarms of insects had (stung, stinged) the campers. _____

▶ **Exercise 3** **Supplying the Correct Forms of Irregular Verbs.** Write the appropriate past or past participle for each verb in parentheses.

EXAMPLE: When inventors first (begin) ___*began*___ to design typewriters, their machines were much different from today's. (began)

(1) In England in 1714, Henry Mill _____ out a patent for a typewriter. (take) (2) However, the records have _____ no details of the machine. (leave) (3) In the United States, William Austin Burt _____ a machine called a "typographer". (build) (4) The machine Burt had _____ was to become the first practical writing machine. (build) (5) As inventors experimented with new designs, the typewriter _____ as large as a piano. (become) (6) However, in 1874 Remington _____ a typewriter out that resembled the modern machine. (put) (7) At first, few businesses _____ the machine. (buy) (8) One drawback was the placement of capital and small letters on separate keyboards, which _____ the speed low. (keep) (9) Another problem was that the typist could not see the paper until it _____ out of the machine. (come) (10) Moreover, when the typist _____ each key, a great deal of pressure was needed. (strike)

21.1 Verb Conjugation • Practice 1

Verb Conjugation   A conjugation is a complete list of the singular and plural forms of a verb. A short conjugation lists just the forms that are used with a single pronoun. As you study the following short conjugations, note that the verbs used with *you* are also used with *we* and *they*. The verbs used with *she*, likewise, are also used with *he* and *it*.

SHORT CONJUGATIONS			
Basic, Progressive and Emphatic	**see (with *I*)**	**see (with *you*)**	**see (with *she*)**
Present	I see	you see	she sees
Past	I saw	you saw	she saw
Future	I will see	you will see	she will see
Present Perfect	I have seen	you have seen	she has seen
Past Perfect	I had seen	you had seen	she had seen
Future Perfect	I will have seen	you will have seen	she will have seen
Present Progressive	I am seeing	you are seeing	she is seeing
Past Progressive	I was seeing	you were seeing	she was seeing
Future Progressive	I will be seeing	you will be seeing	she will be seeing
Present Perfect Progressive	I have been seeing	you have been seeing	she has been seeing
Past Perfect Progressive	I had been seeing	you had been seeing	she had been seeing
Future Perfect Progressive	I will have been seeing	you will have been seeing	she will have been seeing
Present Emphatic	I do see	you do see	she does see
Past Emphatic	I did see	you did see	she did see

▶ **Exercise 1**   **Conjugating Basic and Progressive Forms.**   Complete each of the following short conjugations for all six basic forms and the first three progressive forms.

1. go (with *I*)   2. bring (with *he*)   3. drive (with *we*)   4. turn (with *they*)

_____   _____   _____   _____

_____   _____   _____   _____

_____   _____   _____   _____

_____   _____   _____   _____

_____   _____   _____   _____

_____   _____   _____   _____

_____   _____   _____   _____

_____   _____   _____   _____

_____   _____   _____   _____

▶ **Exercise 2**   **Supplying the Correct Verb Form.**   Fill in each blank with the form of each verb given in parentheses.

EXAMPLE: I _____*was talking*_____ on the phone.   (*talk*, past progressive)

1. Nancy _____ keeping a diary.   (*begin*, present perfect)

2. We _____ on thruways all night.   (*drive*, future perfect progressive)

3. The girls _____ the treasure.   (*find*, past emphatic)

4. The runners _____ on the next pitch.   (*run*, future progressive)

5. A clown's head _____ out of the toy box.   (*spring*, past)

Verb Conjugation • Practice 2

▶ **Exercise 1**   **Conjugating Verbs.**   Conjugate the verbs below in their basic, progressive, and emphatic forms.

1. listen   2. grow

_____   _____

_____   _____

_____   _____

_____   _____

_____   _____

_____   _____

_____   _____

_____   _____

_____

▶ **Writing Application**   **Using Different Tenses.**   Use each verb in a sentence of your own.

EXAMPLE: Past perfect of *read*
            I had read a book yesterday.

1. Future perfect of *leave*

_____

2. Present emphatic of *declare*

_____

3. Past progressive of *use*

_____

4. Future perfect progressive of *walk*

_____

5. Future of *ring*

_____

6. Present of *provoke*

_____

7. Past perfect of *swim*

_____

8. Past perfect progressive of *sing*

_____

9. Future progressive of *cook*

_____

10. Present of *maintain*

_____

21.2 Present, Past, and Future Time • Practice 1

Present, Past, and Future Time   The three forms of the present tense show present actions or conditions as well as various continuous actions or conditions. The seven forms that express past time show actions or conditions beginning in the past. The four forms that express future time show future actions or conditions.

USES OF TENSE IN PRESENT TIME		
Present	present event	I *see* an oriole in that tree.
	recurring event	The bus *is* often late.
	constant event	Water *freezes* at 0°C.
Present Progressive	continuing event	Our neighbors *are building* a porch.
Present Emphatic	emphasizing event	The library *does close* early today.

USES OF TENSE IN PAST TIME		
Past	completed event	The game *started* at 1:00.
Present Perfect	complete (indef. time)	The new mall *has opened*.
	continuing to present	Grandma *has come* to visit.
Past Perfect	completed before another past event	The show *had started* when we got to the theater.
Past Progressive	continuing past event	The leaves *were beginning* to turn.
Present Perfect Progressive	continuing to present	The officials *have been conferring* for a long time now.
Past Perfect Progressive	continuous before another past event	I *had been studying* when the bat flew in the window.
Past Emphatic	emphasized event	I *did leave* the key under the mat.

USES OF TENSE IN FUTURE TIME		
Future	future event	The train *will arrive* shortly.
Future Perfect	future event before another future event	The paint *will have dried* before we need the table.
Future Progressive	continuing future event	The sale *will be continuing* for another five days.
Future Perfect Progressive	continuing before another future event	Next week, the play *will have been running* for five years.

▶ **Exercise 1**   **Identifying Tenses.**   Underline each verb that shows present time. Circle each verb that shows past time. Put parentheses around each verb that shows future time.

EXAMPLE: The police <u>are rerouting</u> all traffic.

1. The caller had hung up by the third ring. _____

2. We will have played each other's team twice by then. _____

3. We did obey all of the contest rules. _____

4. I have been sleepy all day. _____

5. Light travels much faster than sound. _____

6. In about 5 minutes, we will be flying over Pike's Peak. _____

7. A few snowflakes were falling. _____

8. This will be my first ride in a helicopter. _____

9. We had finished dinner just before the blackout. _____

10. Tomorrow night we will be setting the clocks back again. _____

▶ **Exercise 2**   **Identifying Uses of Verbs.**   In the space to the right of each sentence in Exercise 1, write the use of the verb, using the labels in the chart.

EXAMPLE: The police are rerouting all traffic.   *continuing event*

21.2 Present, Past, and Future Time • Practice 2

Exercise 1 **Identifying the Uses of Tense in Present Time.** Identify the use of the verb in each sentence.

1. The bus departs daily from the station at 9:15 A.M. _____

2. Those editorials are promoting an ongoing campaign. _____

3. A cuckoo appears every hour to announce the time. _____

4. Your dinner is ready now. _____

5. A dab of this cologne does seem sufficient. _____

6. Carol is working on an extended project. _____

7. I see two kites in the sky. _____

8. Charles Dickens writes with a melodramatic touch. _____

9. The children are munching on popcorn in the living room. _____

10. Authors are rarely the best critics of their own writing. _____

Exercise 2 **Using Tense in Past Time.** Write the indicated form of each verb in parentheses.

1. I _____ my speech long before it was due.   (write —*past perfect*)

2. Belinda _____ very disagreeable.   (be—*present perfect*)

3. I was startled when the phone suddenly _____.   (ring—*past*)

4. We _____ for a solution to the problem.   (search—*present perfect*)

5. The baby _____ unusually quiet last night.   (be—*past*)

6. This old wicker furniture _____ apart.   (fall—*present perfect*)

7. Bill _____ afraid of heights until he became a paratrooper.   (be—*past perfect*)

8. Susan _____ in the swimming meet.   (compete—*past emphatic*)

9. Fay regretted that she _____ so hastily.   (speak—*past perfect*)

10. We _____ when the lights went out.   (study—*past progressive*)

Exercise 3 **Using Tense in Future Time.** Use an appropriate verb in the form indicated in parentheses to complete each sentence.

1. We _____ at the beach soon.   (action—*future progressive*)

2. By the time she arrives home, the guests _____ for the surprise party. (action—*future perfect*)

3. If the weather is good tomorrow, the children _____ in the dark.   (action—*future*)

4. The doctor said Grandpa _____ better soon.   (condition—*future*)

5. She _____ Europe in the fall.   (action—*future progressive*)

6. By the end of the year, I _____ at the same job for three years.   (action—*future perfect progressive*)

7. My cousin _____ out of school for two weeks by the time my school lets out for the summer.   (condition—*future perfect*)

8. By tonight, I _____ the entire house.   (action—*future perfect*)

9. By opening night, the cast _____ for two months.   (action—*future perfect progressive*)

10. He _____ at his ranch this weekend.   (condition—*future*)

21.2 # Sequence of Tenses • Practice 1

Sequence of Tenses   When showing a sequence of events, do not shift tenses unnecessarily. The tense of a verb in a subordinate clause should follow logically from the tense of the main verb.

SEQUENCE OF TENSES		
Main Verb	**Subordinate Verb**	**Type of Events**
I *think*	that you are making a mistake.	Simultaneous events
I *think*	that you will succeed.	Sequential events
I *thought*	I saw an oriole.	Simultaneous events
I *knew*	that you had left me a key.	Sequential events
I *will see*	who wins the final game.	Simultaneous events (present used as future)
I *will know*	if you have called.	Sequential events

Modifiers That Help Clarify Tense   Use modifiers when they can help to clarify tense.

MODIFIERS THAT CLARIFY TENSE	
I *usually* walk home from school.	*By tonight*, the paint will be dry.

▶ **Exercise 1**   **Using the Correct Tense.**   Rewrite each sentence to improve the sequence of tenses.

EXAMPLE: We were delighted that we are on time.   (simultaneous events)
          We were delighted that we were on time.

1. I will call as soon as I will get there.   (simultaneous events)

   _____

2. They believe that they win on Friday.   (sequential events)

   _____

3. Mom always jogs when she was trying to solve a problem.   (simultaneous events)

   _____

4. We pulled out of the driveway just as he drives up.   (simultaneous events)

   _____

5. I was not surprised that you fail.   (sequential events)

   _____

▶ **Exercise 2**   **Using Modifiers to Help Clarify Tense.**   On each blank, write modifier to clarify the tense. Use a caret [∧] to show where it goes in the sentence.

EXAMPLE: ∧The days get shorter, and the leaves turn.   _____*In the fall*_____

1. The school bus comes late. _____

2. I have been feeling sleepy. _____

3. When we got to the dock, the ferry had left. _____

4. Human beings made tools from stone and pieces of wood. _____

5. Mrs. Costello will take time to help a student with a problem. _____

21.2 Sequence of Tenses • Practice 2

Exercise 1 Using the Correct Forms of Subordinate Verbs, Participles, and Infinitives. Rewrite each sentence, following the instructions in parentheses.

EXAMPLE: I was sorry I spoke so harshly. (Change *spoke* to a perfect infinitive.)
_____I was sorry to have spoken so harshly._____

1. Sally tried growing herbs in the rocky soil. (Change *growing* to a present infinitive.)

_____

2. I understand. (Add a subordinate clause with the present perfect of *be*.)

_____

3. Jeff will be studying hard. (Add a subordinate clause with the present of *learn*.)

_____

4. The campers claimed they saw a grizzly bear. (Change *saw* to a perfect infinitive.)

_____

5. They will find the answer. (Add a subordinate clause with the present of *try*.)

_____

6. He waited for their reaction. (Add a phrase with the perfect participle of *describe*.)

_____

7. We finally reached our destination. (Add a subordinate clause with the past perfect of *travel*.)

_____

8. The director will be making suggestions. (Add a subordinate clause with the present of *perform*.)

_____

9. She remembers only too well. (Add a subordinate clause with the past of *betray*.)

_____

10. The puppy asked for shelter. (Add a phrase with the present participle of *scratch*.)

_____

Exercise 2 Correcting Errors in Tense. Underline unncessary shifts in tense in the following paragraph. Write corrections in the spaces below the paragraph.

(1) *The Little Prince*, a wonderful book by Antoine de Saint-Exupery, is a story that everyone should be reading at least once. (2) It has been narrated by a pilot who must repair his airplane or else have perished on the Sahara Desert. (3) While the pilot had been thus isolated, a little prince from a tiny planet becomes his friend. (4) As the prince will talk about his experiences, the pilot discovered truths for his own life. (5) He will have learned that friendship creates responsibility. (6) He also began to understand that the real essentials are things that are invisible: The most accurate source of vision was the heart. (7) In the end the little prince had returned to his planet, and the pilot's life had never been the same. (8) For him, the stars sometimes sounded like millions of bells. (9) At other times, the bells became tears. (10) But to have understood this, you must first read the book.

_____

_____

_____

_____

_____

21.3 The Subjunctive Mood • Practice 1

The Correct Use of the Subjunctive Mood   Use the subjunctive mood (1) in clauses beginning with *if* or *that* to express an idea contrary to fact or (2) in clauses beginning with *that* to express a request, a demand, or a proposal.

USES OF THE SUBJUNCTIVE	
Ideas Contrary to Fact	**Requests, Demands, Proposals**
I wish that this *were* the first day of vacation, not the last.	The principal asked that Hal *drop* by the office.
If I *were* you, I would not tell her.	The contest rules specify that entries *be* neat.
	I move that the meeting *be adjourned.*

▶ **Exercise 1**   **Using the Subjunctive Mood.**   Rewrite each sentence, changing the verb that should be in the subjunctive mood to its correct form.

EXAMPLE: It is imperative that he takes the next plane.
 _____It is imperative that he take the next plane._____

1. If it was possible to help him, I would do it.

   _____

2. The law requires that you are sixteen before you can ride a moped.

   _____

3. My boss insists that I am punctual.

   _____

4. Grandpa treats me as if I was still a baby.

   _____

5. The committee voted that the proposal is shelved.

   _____

6. Mrs. Minnow requests that anyone needing a ride sees her before noon today.

   _____

7. I wish that I was rich.

   _____

8. The captain requests that everyone remains seated till the plane stops.

   _____

9. I wish that I was you, taking a trip like that!

   _____

10. The judge ordered that the defendant pays a fine.

    _____

▶ **Exercise 2**   **Writing Sentences Using the Subjunctive Mood.**   Write a sentence using each item. Make sure that each sentence contains a verb in the subjunctive mood.

EXAMPLE: asked that   ___The jury asked that the judge explain the new law.___

1. I move that _____

2. If I were _____

3. insists that _____

4. require that _____

5. that he be _____

21.3 The Subjunctive Mood • Practice 2

Exercise 1 **Using the Subjunctive Mood.** Rewrite each sentence, changing the verb that should be in the subjunctive mood to the subjunctive mood.

EXAMPLE: She suggests that Paula gives her speech now.
   She suggests that Paula give her speech now.

1. If there was a concert tonight, we would go.

   _____

2. I wish that I was free to choose.

   _____

3. The teacher prefers that Elizabeth sits in the front row.

   _____

4. The law requires that you are sixteen before you drive.

   _____

5. Her grandparents propose that she stays with them.

   _____

6. I wish that I was more imaginative.

   _____

7. She spoke to him as if he was a child.

   _____

8. The judge ordered that the defendant stands trial tomorrow.

   _____

9. The boy shrieked as if the shadow he saw was a monster.

   _____

10. He would prefer that his son goes to a military school.

   _____

Writing Application **Writing Sentences Using the Subjunctive Mood.** Use each item in a sentence containing a verb in the subjunctive mood.

1. suggest that

   _____

2. were to see

   _____

3. if I were

   _____

4. that you be

   _____

5. that you write

   _____

Name _____ Date _____

Active and Passive Voice   A verb is active if its subject performs the action. A verb is passive if its action is performed upon the subject.

Active Voice	Passive Voice
The storm damaged the pine tree.	The pine tree was damaged by the storm.
My mother painted that landscape.	That landscape was painted by my mother.

A passive verb is made from a form of *be* plus the past participle of a transitive verb.

THE VERB *ELECT* IN THE PASSIVE VOICE		
Tense	**Basic Forms**	**Progressive Form**
Present	I am elected	I am being elected
Past	I was elected	I was being elected
Future	I will be elected	
Present Perfect	I have been elected	
Past Perfect	I had been elected	
Future Perfect	I will have been elected	

▶ **Exercise 1**   **Distinguishing Between Active and Passive Voice.**   After each sentence, write *active* or *passive* to describe the verb.

EXAMPLE: The police have already been notified. _____*passive*_____

1. A strange car was parked in our driveway. _____
2. The letter carrier left a large package for you. _____
3. Nancy's nomination was seconded by Luis. _____
4. Detective Sharp examined the chain of paper clips with interest. _____
5. The firm was founded by Alec's grandfather in 1912. _____
6. By this weekend, a new Homecoming Queen will have been chosen. _____
7. These peaches have been bruised. _____
8. The damaged airliner landed safely. _____
9. Aunt Betsy taught Ellen and me how to play golf. _____
10. Waldo's new book is being praised by the critics. _____

▶ **Exercise 2**   **Forming the Tenses of Passive Verbs.**   Write the passive forms indicated.

EXAMPLE: future of *remember* (with *she*) _____*she will be remembered*_____

1. past of *disappoint* (with *we*) _____
2. past perfect of *injure* (with *he*) _____
3. past progressive of *consult* (with *they*) _____
4. present of *remind* (with *I*) _____
5. present perfect of *report* (with *it*) _____
6. future of *select* (with *she*) _____
7. present progressive of *build* (with *it*) _____
8. present of *honor* (with *I*) _____
9. past of *invite* (with *you*) _____
10. future of *publish* (with *it*) _____

21.4 Active and Passive Voice • Practice 2

▶ **Exercise 1** **Distinguishing Between the Active and Passive Voice.** Identify each verb as *active* or *passive*.

EXAMPLE: The man was given a harsh sentence by the judge. ___*passive*___

1. His bizarre behavior was ridiculed by his peers. _____
2. This wildlife sanctuary protects endangered species. _____
3. The senior class will collect money for a field trip. _____
4. This new film is praised by the critics for its honesty. _____
5. Mr. Schwartz is opening a new store in this area. _____
6. By tonight the letter will have been read by the committee. _____
7. The two astronauts floated in outer space. _____
8. Bill is being called up for jury duty. _____
9. Reporters swarmed around the scene of the crime. _____
10. The butler slowly opened the door. _____
11. The story about Big Foot is being investigated by a team of
    naturalists. _____
12. The letter was typed by Greg on his new word processor. _____
13. The announcements about school closings will be made on a local radio
    station. _____
14. You must groom your dog carefully before the contest. _____
15. A pathway to the garage was being shoveled by my brother. _____
16. Susan will have returned from her vacation by now. _____
17. The winner was given a certificate by the mayor. _____
18. Those trees were planted by the previous owners. _____
19. A Brazilian architect designed this plaza. _____
20. We spotted a blue jay in the oak tree yesterday. _____

▶ **Exercise 2** **Forming the Tenses of Passive Verbs.** Conjugate each verb in the passive voice.

1. elect (with *I*)

   _____

2. prepare (with *you*)

   _____

3. know (with *she*)

   _____

4. give (with *we*)

   _____

Name _____   Date _____

 21.4 # Using Voice • **Practice 1**

Use active voice whenever possible. It is usually more direct and economical than the passive voice.

Active Voice	Passive Voice
The Penguins won the tournament.	The tournament was won by the Penguins.

Use the passive voice to emphasize the receiver of an action rather than the performer of an action. Also use the passive to point out the receiver of an action whenever the performer is not important or not easily identified.

Emphasizing the Receiver	Performer Unknown or Unimportant
A child *was bitten* by the dog.	The soldier *was killed* in action.
The speaker *was interrupted* by hecklers.	The letter *was opened* by mistake.

▶ **Exercise 1**   **Using the Active and Passive Voice.**   Five of the passive sentences below would be more forceful in the active voice. Write *weak* after each sentence of this kind. Five sentences are acceptable because they emphasize the receiver of the action or because the performer is unimportant or unknown. Write *acceptable* after these passive sentences.

EXAMPLE: A winner has been selected by the judges. _____*weak*_____
            This radio was made in Japan. _____*acceptable*_____

1. The car was quickly sold by the owner. _____
2. The metric system is used throughout most of the world. _____
3. One student's name was accidentally omitted from the list. _____
4. The early settlers were alarmed by the severe winter. _____
5. Last night our car was stolen. _____
6. Several islands were destroyed by the volcanic eruption. _____
7. The playwright was urged by the director to rewrite the last act. _____
8. My best friend has been chosen for that role. _____
9. William the Conqueror was crowned on Christmas Day. _____
10. All cars on Route 9 are being stopped by state troopers. _____

▶ **Exercise 2**   **Correcting Weak Passive Sentences.**   Rewrite the five sentences you labeled weak in Exercise 1 above. Change or add words as necessary to put each verb into the active voice.

EXAMPLE: _____*The judges have selected a winner.*_____

1. _____
2. _____
3. _____
4. _____
5. _____

21.4 Using Voice • Practice 2

▶**Exercise 1** **Using the Active Voice.** The following sentences have verbs in the passive voice. Rewrite each sentence, changing or adding words as necessary in order to put each verb into the active voice.

EXAMPLE: The man was given a harsh sentence by the judge.
        The judge gave the man a harsh sentence.

1. The paper was written by Georgia.

   _____

2. The reports were presented by the students.

   _____

3. The football was thrown by the quarterback for more than forty yards.

   _____

4. The concert was attended by thousands of fans.

   _____

5. The lightning storm was watched by the people in the restaurant.

   _____

6. This painting was done by Vincent van Gogh.

   _____

7. The story was read with great expression by the children's librarian.

   _____

8. The gifts were opened by Gloria and me.

   _____

9. The meal was enjoyed by the hungry children.

   _____

10. "The Jilting of Granny Weatherall" was written by Katherine Anne Porter.

   _____

▶**Exercise 2** **Correcting Unnecessary Use of the Passive Voice.** Rewrite the following paragraph, changing at least five uses of the passive to active.

   (1) Her mother had been buried three days. (2) Now, standing in her mother's kitchen, Emma was made uneasy by the heavy silence of the house. (3) What already dulled memory of sound was being forgotten? (4) Then she remembered. (5) A black cloth hung over the cage, where it had been placed many evenings ago. (6) Inside, shrouded in darkness, would be the canary, a birthday present that had been gleefully given to her mother by the grandchildren. (7) Death was so unfair. (8) But the bird still lived. (9) As the cloth slid to the floor, the canary's head was untucked from its wing. (10) Its slight body was shaken with a weak but persistent song of life.

   _____

   _____

   _____

   _____

   _____

   _____

   _____

22.1 Case • Practice 1

The Three Cases   Case is a form of a noun or pronoun that indicates its use in a sentence. The three cases are the nominative, the objective, and the possessive. Pronouns often have different forms for all three cases. Nouns change form only to show the possessive case.

Case	Use in Sentence	Forms
Nominative	subject, predicate nominative	I; you; he, she, it; we, they; teacher, teachers
Objective	direct object, indirect object, object of a preposition, object of a verbal	me; you; him, her, it; us, them; teacher, teachers
Possessive	to show ownership	my, mine; your, yours; his, her, hers, its; our, ours; their, theirs; teacher's, teachers'

> **Exercise 1**   **Identifying Case.**   Write the case of each underlined noun or pronoun in the following sentences.

EXAMPLE: Is this notebook <u>yours</u>?   _____possessive_____

1. The magician explained the trick to Steve and <u>me</u>. _____
2. <u>We</u> finished the job in no time. _____
3. The woman jogging on the beach is <u>she</u>. _____
4. Our <u>neighbors'</u> house was damaged by the storm. _____
5. By rights, the reward should be <u>hers</u> alone. _____
6. <u>Their</u> customs are much different from ours. _____
7. The storm changed <u>its</u> course and went out to sea. _____
8. We would have done better if we had followed the <u>coach's</u> advice. _____
9. You can buy apples at the stand or pick <u>them</u> yourself. _____
10. The suitcase with the red tag on it is <u>mine</u>. _____

> **Exercise 2**   **Recognizing the Use of Nouns and Pronouns.**   After each number, write the use of each underlined noun and pronoun in Exercise 1. Write one of the following: *subject, predicate nominative, direct object, indirect object, object of a preposition,* or *to show ownership*.

EXAMPLE: _____to show ownership_____

1. _____
2. _____
3. _____
4. _____
5. _____

6. _____
7. _____
8. _____
9. _____
10. _____

22.1 Case • Practice 2

▶ **Exercise 1** **Identifying Case.** Write the case of each underlined pronoun. Then write its use.

EXAMPLE: Sheila gave <u>him</u> two tickets for the concert. ___*objective*   *(indirect object)*___

1. <u>Her</u> staunch support has not gone unnoticed. _____
2. The exam should cause <u>him</u> no difficulty. _____
3. It seems that we and <u>they</u> have much in common. _____
4. Before you use the computer, ask <u>them</u> for a demonstration. _____
5. We were pleased to use <u>their</u> cabin for the weekend. _____
6. Sally made this dragon kite for you and <u>me</u>. _____
7. Surely <u>you</u> will be able to solve the problem. _____
8. I meant to give <u>you</u> this money yesterday. _____
9. When the car would not start, we had to leave <u>it</u> at home in the
   garage. _____
10. Hiding <u>them</u> made him an accessory to the crime. _____
11. After Jean arrived, we told <u>her</u> the secret. _____
12. Is this book John's or <u>yours</u>? _____
13. Please allow <u>me</u> to make the decision. _____
14. The ushers at the wedding will be Ted and <u>I</u>. _____
15. Apologetically, the waitress served <u>us</u> the cold soup. _____
16. The responsibility for this negligence is <u>ours</u> alone. _____
17. <u>We</u> tilled the fields without any assistance. _____
18. The swimming team captain will be either Monica or <u>she</u>. _____
19. A full moon cast <u>its</u> soft light on the ground below. _____
20. In our opinion the best fashion designer is <u>he</u>. _____

▶ **Exercise 2** **Identifying Case and Use.** On the line, write the case and use of each underlined pronoun in the paragraphs. Possible uses include subject, predicate nominative, direct object, indirect object, object of a preposition, or to show ownership.

EXAMPLE: ___*he*   *(nominative case)*   *(subject)*___

   Julianne and Timothy stood in the darkness of <u>their</u> own backyard and looked up at the moon. "What a gorgeous night!" exclaimed Julianne. Timothy turned to look at <u>her</u>, smiling <u>his</u> agreement.
   The loud, insistent ringing of <u>their</u> phone interrupted <u>them</u>. Expecting an important call, Timothy ran into the house, walked over to the phone, and picked <u>it</u> up. "Timothy Rogers?" asked a voice <u>he</u> recognized instantly.
   "This is <u>he</u>," said Timothy, looking at Julianne, who was just coming in the door. <u>He</u> gave <u>her</u> a quick wink and the thumbs-up sign.

1. _____   6. _____
2. _____   7. _____
3. _____   8. _____
4. _____   9. _____
5. _____   10. _____

22.1 Nominative Case and Objective Case
• Practice 1

The Nominative Case   Use the nominative case for the subject of a verb, for a predicate nominative, and for the pronoun at the beginning of a nominative absolute.

USES OF NOMINATIVE PRONOUNS	
Subject	*We* are just about to leave.
Predicate Nominative	The first one chosen should have been *she*.
Nominative Absolute	*He* being my best friend, I hated to report him.

The Objective Case   Use the objective case for the object of any verb, verbal, or preposition, or for the subject of an infinitive.

USES OF OBJECTIVE PRONOUNS	
Object	The pitcher struck *him* out. (of a verb)
	After chopping *them*, brown the onions. (of a verbal)
Indirect Object	We got *her* a get-well card.
Object of the Preposition	We enjoyed our visit with *them*.
Subject of Infinitive	John asked *us* to have dinner with him.

▶ **Exercise 1**   **Identifying Pronouns in the Nominative Case.**   Circle the pronoun in the nominative case to complete each sentence. Then indicate the use of the pronoun by writing *S* (subject), *PN* (predicate nominative), or *NA* (pronoun in a nominative absolute).

EXAMPLE: The girl in the on-deck circle is (⟨she⟩, her).   *PN*

1. It was (she, her) whom the voters believed. _____

2. The owners of the sailboat are the Hellers and (them, they). _____

3. Elena and (her, she) had met several years before. _____

4. Ed decided against eating out, (his, he) being short of cash. _____

5. Both Greg and (her, she) are excellent storytellers. _____

▶ **Exercise 2**   **Identifying Pronouns in the Objective Case.**   Circle the pronoun in the objective case to complete each sentence. Then indicate the pronoun's use as *DO* (direct object of a verb or verbal), *IO* (indirect object), *OP* (object of the preposition), or *SI* (subject of an infinitive).

EXAMPLE: The principal asked (I, ⟨me⟩) to come to his office.   *SI*

1. Thank you for helping (we, us) out. _____

2. I will take that package along with (I, me). _____

3. We invited Jill and (him, he) to come along, too. _____

4. They asked (she, her) to sing at commencement. _____

5. Paul sent Joe and (her, she) a postcard from Rhode Island. _____

6. I have trouble choosing among (they, them). _____

7. We tried to convince Martha and (she, her). _____

8. The class chose (they, them) to represent our school. _____

9. We all want (her, she) to succeed at her new job. _____

10. The star gave (I, me) her autograph after the performance. _____

22.1 Nominative Case and Objective Case
• Practice 2

Exercise 1 **Identifying Pronouns in the Nominative Case.** Underline the pronoun in the nominative case to complete each sentence. Then write the use of the pronoun.

1. Paul and (me, I) will make our presentation first. _____
2. Charlene and (he, him) deserve credit for our victory. _____
3. The ones to decide are (us, we) committee members. _____
4. (She, Her) having announced a recess, everyone left. _____
5. (He, Him) and Amy collaborated on that book. _____
6. Harold and (they, them) were sent to help the refugees. _____
7. Carla and (I, me) are studying Russian. _____
8. I could not find Ed, (he, him) having left after class. _____
9. The best sailors on this lake are (we, us) boys. _____
10. Both Marc and (her, she) are good at pantomime. _____

Exercise 2 **Using Pronouns in the Nominative Case.** Write a nominative pronoun to complete each sentence. Then write the use of the pronoun.

1. You and _____ cannot lift the crate by ourselves. _____
2. It is _____ who should be held accountable. _____
3. Mr. Levitt's new receptionist will be _____. _____
4. Two representatives at the convention will be he and _____. _____
5. Esther and _____ were always my favorite aunts. _____

Exercise 3 **Identifying Pronouns in the Objective Case.** Underline the pronoun in the objective case to complete each sentence. Then write the use of the pronoun.

1. The map was drawn by Lee and (I, me). _____
2. They asked Carol and (he, him) to babysit tonight. _____
3. Bentley sent (them, they) to inspect the summer cottage. _____
4. A lifeguard tried to warn Philip and (her, she). _____
5. Jackie sent (him, he) the picture of her family. _____
6. The chimpanzee grinned at my brother and (I, me). _____
7. Jules sat between Cynthia and (I, me). _____
8. Give (us, we) students a chance before you reject the idea. _____
9. I would like to recommend Michelle and (he, him). _____
10. The man helping (us, we) was Ted's father. _____

Exercise 4 **Using Pronouns in the Objective Case.** Write an objective pronoun to complete each sentence. Then write the use of the pronoun.

1. This hat must have been designed with _____ in mind. _____
2. We often think about Uncle Wilbur and _____. _____
3. Leaving _____ by themselves may be a mistake. _____
4. Their parents brought _____ numerous souvenirs. _____
5. When can we expect _____ to arrive? _____

Possessive Case • Practice 1

Errors to Avoid with Possessive Pronouns   Use the possessive case before gerunds. Avoid using an apostrophe with possessive pronouns, and do not confuse possessive pronouns with contractions.

AVOIDING ERRORS WITH POSSESSIVE PRONOUNS	
Correct	Incorrect
His complaining bothered everyone.	*Him* complaining bothered everyone.
Their shouting was quite distracting.	*They're* shouting was quite distracting.
Its appearance was horrifying.	*It's* appearance was horrifying.
It's going to be a great game.	*Its* going to be a great game.

 **Exercise 1**   **Using Pronouns in the Possessive Case.**   Underline the correct word in each set of parentheses.

EXAMPLE: (Their, They're) friends all showed up.

1. (Her, She) crying made everyone feel sad.
2. (It's, Its) going to be a difficult test.
3. That is (my, mine) house.
4. (Him, His) winning amazed all of the other players in the tournament.
5. (They're, Their) going to accept responsibility for their actions.
6. (Our, Us) singing entertained everyone who attended the party.
7. (Its, It's) value is impossible to determine.
8. (My, Mine) shoes are on the couch.
9. The shoes on the couch are (my, mine).
10. Bob was really angered by (our, us) bickering.
11. We were surprised at (him, his) returning so soon.
12. The fault is at least partly (theirs, their's).
13. With (him, his) quitting in midseason, the team was left without a coach.
14. Each of these pigeons has (its, it's) own markings.
15. I am very happy with (my, mine) choice.

Exercise 2   **Using all Three Cases of Pronouns.**   Underline the correct word in each set of parentheses.

EXAMPLE: The big surprise was (me, my) getting an A on the test.

1. This is the first year that Tom and (me, I) have been on the same team.
2. (Him, His) playing the trumpet at night annoyed the neighbors.
3. We wanted Nancy and (her, she) to come with us.
4. You can recognize the black widow spider by (it's, its) markings.
5. Let's keep this a secret between you and (me, I).
6. Which pair of skates is (yours, your's)?
7. If anyone should be punished, it is (she, her).
8. It was (him, his) blocking the punt that won the game.
9. (They're, Their) protesting the umpire's call was futile.
10. Neither Beth nor (she, her) had heard the announcement.

22.1 Possessive Case • Practice 2

▶**Exercise 1** **Using Pronouns in the Possessive Case.** Underline the correct word in each set of parentheses.

1. I don't know whether this book is John's or (hers, her's).
2. (Him, His) talking in class is bothering everyone.
3. The mustang had broken out of (it's, its) corral.
4. (Their, They're) not likely to approve this proposal.
5. That gazebo could only be (theirs, their's).
6. (Its, It's) time that he took more responsibility.
7. This model airplane is (mine, mine's).
8. (Their, They're) excuses were ridiculous.
9. (Our, Us) complaining only got us into trouble.
10. The defendant couldn't prove the ring was (hers, her's).

▶**Writing Application** **Writing Sentences with Nominative, Objective, and Possessive Pronouns.** Use the following instructions to write ten sentences of your own.

1. Use *she and I* as the subject of a verb.

_____

2. Use *our* before a gerund.

_____

3. Use *them* as a direct object.

_____

4. Use *you and me* as the object of a preposition.

_____

5. Use *he* as part of a nominative absolute construction.

_____

6. Use *we* followed by an appositive as the subject of a verb.

_____

7. Use *theirs* after linking verb.

_____

8. Use *us* as an indirect object followed by an appositive.

_____

9. Use *me* as the subject of an infinitive.

_____

10. Use *he and they* as a compound predicate nominative.

_____

22.2 # Special Problems With Pronouns • **Practice 1**

Using *Who and Whom* Correctly   Learn to recognize the cases of *who* and *whom* and to use them correctly in sentences. *Who* and *whoever* are in the nominative case and are used for subjects and predicate nominatives. *Whom* and *whomever* are in the objective case and are used for direct objects and objects of prepositions. For the possessive case, use *whose*, not *who's*.

CORRECT USE OF *WHO* AND *WHOM*	
Nominative	*Who* knows the answer?
	Whoever has the lowest score wins.
	The detective discovered *who* the murderer was.
Objective	*Whom* have you invited so far?
	To *whom* did you give the message?
Possessive	*Whose* notebook is this?

Pronouns in Elliptical Clauses   In elliptical clauses beginning with *than* or *as*, use the form of the pronoun that you would use if the clauses were fully stated.

Elliptical Clauses	Completed Clauses
Paul is taller than ____?____ .	Paul is taller than she [is].
The news surprised Ben as well as ____?____ .	The news surprised Ben as well as [it surprised] me.

▷**Exercise 1**   **Using Who and Whom Correctly.**   Complete each sentence by writing *who, whom, whoever,* or *whomever.*

EXAMPLE: ____*Who*____ was elected president in 1960?

1. Give the message to _____ is in the office.

2. The candidate _____ we supported won the election.

3. To _____ did you report the accident?

4. Laurie is a person _____ knows what she wants.

5. _____ wrote this story had a good sense of humor.

6. Do you know _____ the judges selected?

7. _____, in your opinion, committed the murder?

8. _____ has the team chosen as captain?

9. Anyone _____ witnessed the accident should contact the police.

10. There are still a few actors _____ the director has not auditioned.

▷**Exercise 2**   **Using Pronouns in Elliptical Clauses.**   Complete each sentence with an appropriate pronoun from the parentheses.

EXAMPLE: Nick is nearly as tall as ____*I*____ . (I, me)

1. The teacher gave Elena a higher final grade than _____ . (I, me)

2. Can you run the mile faster than _____ ? (she, her)

3. The postman brought more mail for them than _____ . (we, us)

4. Dad found the incident more embarrassing than _____ . (I, we)

5. Ed has a quicker temper than _____ . (she, her)

22.2 Special Problems With Pronouns • Practice 2

> **Exercise 1**   **Using Who and Whom Correctly in Questions.**   Underline the correct pronoun in each sentence.

1. (Who, Whom) did Ed ask for a ride?
2. (Who, Whom) would support such a cause?
3. From (who, whom) did you receive that gift?
4. The participants were (who, whom)?
5. (Who, Whom) will be successful in balancing the budget?
6. (Who, Whom) was chosen for the lead in *Richard III*?
7. (Whoever, Whomever) could have left these flowers?
8. To (who, whom) did you send the telegram?
9. (Who, Whom) were you supposed to follow in the caravan?
10. Can you tell me (who, whom) I must see about this matter?

> **Exercise 2**   **Using *Who* and *Whom* Correctly in Clauses.**   Underline the subordinate clause in each sentence. Then indicate how the form of *who* or *whom* is used in that clause.

EXAMPLE: I want to know who wrote this.   *subject*

1. We thanked the boy who delivered the groceries. _____
2. We could not determine whom he meant. _____
3. Give the message to whoever is at home. _____
4. Sidney flattered whoever would help him. _____
5. This man is a sharp-tongued cynic whom I dislike. _____
6. Whomever he selects will have a difficult task. _____
7. Only those who are hard-working need apply. _____
8. She is the one who, I suspect, will be most capable. _____
9. Barry did not know whom he could confide in. _____
10. The mechanic who fixed our car is the best in town. _____

> **Exercise 3**   **Identifying the Correct Pronoun in Elliptical Clauses.**   Rewrite each sentence, choosing the correct pronoun in parentheses and completing the elliptical clauses.

1. This flutist has a better tone than (he, him).

_____

2. You are more perceptive than (she, her).

_____

3. Old memories mean more to me than to (he, him).

_____

4. Nancy earns more money than (he, him).

_____

5. She was as delighted as (I, me).

_____

23.1 Agreement With Singular and Plural Subjects • Practice 1

The Number of Nouns, Pronouns, and Verbs   Number refers to the two forms of a word: singular and plural. Singular words indicate one; plural words indicate more than one.

	NUMBER OF WORDS		
Part of Speech	**Singular**	**Plural**	**Singular or Plural**
Nouns	factory child	factories children	deer, moose, sheep
Pronoun	I, he, she, it	we, they	you
Verbs	am, is, was has, does likes, goes		(You, we, they) are, were (I, you, we, they) have, do (I, you, we, they) like, go

Singular and Plural Subjects   A singular subject must have a singular verb. A plural subject must have a plural verb. A phrase or clause that interrupts a subject and its verb does not affect subject-verb agreement.

SUBJECT-VERB AGREEMENT	
Singular	**Plural**
She likes chow mein.	We like chop suey.
A box of dishes has fallen off the moving van.	The dishes in the box are not broken.

▷ **Exercise 1**   **Determining the Number of Words.**   Identify each item as *S* (singular), *P* (plural), or *both*.

EXAMPLE: you ____*both*____

1. it _____
2. moose _____
3. has gone _____
4. laundry _____
5. children _____

6. praise _____
7. sheep _____
8. ignores _____
9. teach _____
10. forgot _____

▷ **Exercise 2**   **Making Subjects and Verbs Agree.**   Complete each sentence by writing the verb form in the parentheses that agrees with the subject.

EXAMPLE: The cost of the new weapons ____*is*____ staggering.   (is, are)

1. Several severe storms in early summer _____ endangered crops.   (has, have)

2. Sammy, my favorite of all the mice, _____ finally mastered the maze. (has, have)

3. The candidate, along with her assistants, _____ writing a speech.   (is, are)

4. Mary, who loves to wear bright green clothes, _____ pale blue eyes.   (has, have)

5. The four parts of the treasure map _____ been pasted together.   (has, have)

23.1 Subject and Verb Agreement With Singular and Plural Subjects • Practice 2

▷ **Exercise 1** **Determine the Number of Nouns, Pronouns, and Verbs.** Identify each item as *singular, plural,* or *both.*

EXAMPLE: crawls _____singular_____

1. sits _____
2. mouse _____
3. gloves _____
4. speech _____
5. they _____

6. has lost _____
7. trembled _____
8. were _____
9. was simmering _____
10. begin _____

▷ **Exercise 2** **Making Subjects Agree with Their Verbs.** Underline the verb in parentheses that agrees with the subject of each sentence.

1. Overhead fans (was, were) circulating the warm air.
2. My turtle (lives, live) exclusively on flies.
3. An artesian well (provides, provide) all the water we need.
4. I (objects, object) to doing manual labor.
5. The stainless steel pans (lasts, last) for a lifetime.

▷ **Exercise 3** **Making Separated Subjects and Verbs Agree.** Underline the verb in parentheses that agrees with the subject of each sentence.

1. Peter, along with his brothers, (goes, go) skating often.
2. The pages of the letter, yellowed with age, (was, were) filled with beautiful handwriting.
3. A falconer, a person who works with hawks, (is, are) now an uncommon sight.
4. This painting, just like that one, (costs, cost) far less.
5. Rocks formed from molten magma (is, are) igneous.
6. My sister, accompanied by my mother, (has, have) bought her first pair of designer jeans.
7. Tomorrow the first customer, whoever that may be, (is, are) going to receive a gift certificate.
8. The lamp, which was broken, now (work, works) properly.
9. The leader of the troops (expects, expect) to be obeyed.
10. A child who is ignored (expects, expect) little of others.

▷ **Exercise 4** **Making Relative Pronouns Agree With Their Verbs.** Underline the verb in the parentheses that agrees with the subject of each subordinate clause.

1. Kathleen is popular with those classmates who (enjoy, enjoys) her vitality and exuberance.
2. Some of these snakes, which (is, are) all poisonous, are milked for their venom.
3. State health regulations apply to all employees in this establishment who (handles, handle) food.
4. Every book on these shelves that (appears, appear) on your list should be cataloged.
5. I am one of the many people who (lives, live) for tomorrow.
6. Only those puppies from the litter that (exhibits, exhibit) aggressive behavior will be trained guard dogs.
7. A lady slipper is a kind of orchid that (grows, grow) in acid soil in the northern United States.
8. Bob is the one person who (know, knows) the answer.
9. Any student who (wants, want) help should see Mr. Barton.
10. Lyle is a hard worker with many relatives who (count, counts) on him for financial support.

Name _____   Date _____

 23.1 # Agreement With Compound Subjects
• Practice 1

Compound Subjects   A singular subject after *or* takes a singular verb. A plural subject after *or* takes a plural verb. Compound subjects joined by *and* take a plural verb unless they are thought of as one thing or modified by *every* or *each*.

AGREEMENT WITH COMPOUND SUBJECTS	
Joined by *or* or *nor*	The manager or her assistant *is* usually in the store.
	Neither the library nor the courthouse *is* open on Sunday.
	An apple or grapes *make* a good snack.
	Grapes or an apple *makes* a good snack.
Joined by *and*	String beans, peas, and soybeans *are* legumes.
	The catcher and the pitcher *make* up the battery.
	Spaghetti and meatballs *is* my favorite dish.
	Every suitcase and parcel *was* inspected at the gate.

▶ **Exercise 1**   **Compound Subjects Joined by *Or* or *Nor*.**   Write the verb form in parentheses that agrees with the subject in each sentence.

EXAMPLE: A rubber band or a big paper clip _____*is*_____ what you need. (is, are)

1. A nurse or an aide usually _____ patients' temperatures. (takes, take)

2. Neither the players nor the coach _____ anything to regret.   (has, have)

3. A wok or a frying pan _____ essential for cooking this dish.   (is, are)

4. Coffee, tea, or milk _____ each meal.   (accompanies, accompany)

5. Neither the directions nor the example _____ clear.   (was, were)

6. Nicole, Chris, or Tom _____ let the dog back in.   (has, have)

7. Soup or dessert _____ extra.   (costs, cost)

8. Either a hamster or gerbil _____ a good pet.   (makes, make)

9. Neither Mrs. Kokoros nor her children _____ much Greek.   (speaks, speak)

10. A pen or pencil in the glove compartment often _____ in handy.   (comes, come)

▶ **Exercise 2**   **Compound Subjects Joined by *And*.**   Write the verb form in parentheses that agrees with the subject in each sentence.

EXAMPLE: Chicken and dumplings _____*is*_____ the Blue Plate Special. (is, are)

1. Tornadoes and thunderstorms _____ rare at this time of year.   (is, are)

2. Pears and cheese _____ well together.   (goes, go)

3. Each soldier and sailor _____ given a free pass.   (was, were)

4. Both management and the union _____ that the contract is fair.   (agrees, agree)

5. The post office and banks _____ on Columbus Day.   (closes, close)

6. The hotel and that office tower _____ recent additions.   (is, are)

7. Ham and eggs _____ my favorite breakfast.   (is, are)

8. Pliers and screwdriver _____ needed to assemble the bike.   (is, are)

9. Every teacher and student in the school _____ contributed.   (has, have)

10. Both Lisa and her mother _____ tennis.   (enjoys, enjoy)

23.1 Agreement With Compound Subjects
• Practice 2

▶ **Exercise 1**   **Making Compound Subjects Agree With Their Verbs.**   Underline the verb in the parentheses that agrees with the subject of each sentence.

1. A tent and a sleeping bag (is, are) the equipment you need.
2. Each boy and girl (wear, wears) a dark blue uniform.
3. Neither Dan nor Kay (is, are) going to the concert.
4. A squirrel and several mice (reside, resides) in the attic.
5. Rayon and nylon (is, are) synthetic fabrics.
6. A few children or one adult (raises, raise) the flag.
7. Eddie or Maria (give, gives) tours of the old mansion.
8. Their sons or daughters often (helps, help) with the meals.
9. Spaghetti and meatballs (is, are) a Friday night special.
10. The niece or the nephew (is, are) taking care of her.
11. Either the students or their representative (attends, attend) each meeting.
12. Two cars or a van (is, are) needed for the outing.
13. Either Kim or Barry (is, are) organizing the ceremony.
14. The twins or Alex (prepare, prepares) the evening meal.
15. Mr. Rolf or the Thayers (shovels, shovel) the snow.
16. Neither Rick nor Amy (knows, know) the route to the cabin.
17. Pork and beans (was, were) served at the party.
18. Neither the hotel nor the two motels (was, were) quiet.
19. Every junior and senior (was, were) invited to the party.
20. Neither the flight attendants nor the pilot (knows, know) how to calm the frightened passengers.

▶ **Exercise 2**   **Making Verbs Agree with Compound Subjects.**   Write the verb form in the parentheses that agrees with the compound subject in each sentence. Then underline the compound subject.

EXAMPLE: Many cars and trucks _____*speed*_____ (speeds, speed) past the exit.

Fiona and Mabel _____ (goes, go) to the movies every Saturday. Neither popcorn

nor soda _____ (is, are) purchased by the girls. Instead, mineral water and

pizza _____ (satisfies, satisfy) their desires for snacks. The snack-bar attendants and

the ticket takers all _____ (expects, expect) to see Fiona and Mabel on Saturday.

Sometimes, Barney and Adam _____ (accompanies, accompany) the girls. Popcorn

and chocolate _____ (is, are) the favorite snacks of the boys.

Fiona and Mabel _____ (prefers, prefer) movies that are either funny or

romantic. Barney and Adam _____ (likes, like) science fiction and adventure movies.

The four friends and their dogs often _____ (takes, take) a long walk later in the day.

Fido and Lance _____ (barks, bark) at every passing car, but the girls' dogs are much

better behaved.

Name _____ Date _____

23.1 Agreement With Confusing Subjects
• Practice 1

Confusing Subjects Always check certain kinds of subjects carefully to make sure they agree with their verbs.

AGREEMENT WITH CONFUSING SUBJECTS	
Subject After Verb	There *is* only one more *lot* left on our street.
	Within each one of us *lies* secret *fear*.
Subject Versus Predicate Nominative	My favorite *dessert* is peaches with cream.
	Chocolate chip *cookies are* one of my weaknesses.
Plural Form with Singular Meaning	*Mumps is* a serious illness in an adult.
	Gymnastics is growing in popularity.
Amounts and Measurements	Two *months sounds* like a long time to be away.
	Three *cups* of sugar *is* too much for that recipe.
Titles	*Wuthering Heights was* as good a movie as a book.
Indefinite Pronouns	*Either* of the twins *is* a capable sitter. (always singular)
	Several of my classmates *have* cars. (always plural)
	Some of the cheese *is* spoiled.
	Some of the bananas *are* too ripe.
Collective Nouns	The *class has* chosen its officers. (as a group)
	The *class have* finished their reports. (individually)

▶ **Exercise 1** **Deciding on the Number of Subjects.** Assume that each item below is to be the subject of a sentence. Label each one *S* if it needs a singular verb or *P* if it needs a plural verb.

EXAMPLE: *Jo's Boys*   S

1. Some of the cars _____
2. Economics _____
3. *The Brothers Karamazov* _____
4. All of the pie _____
5. Measles _____
6. Each of the students _____
7. *Sense and Sensibility* _____
8. Mathematics _____
9. Either of the plans _____
10. Some of the corn _____

▶ **Exercise 2** **Choosing Verbs to Agree with Difficult Subjects.** Write the correct verb form from parentheses to complete each sentence.

EXAMPLE: Here ____is____ the sweater you lent me. (is, are)

1. The concert series _____ tomorrow night.   (begins, begin)
2. The committee _____ arguing among themselves about the plan.   (is, are)
3. Along the coast _____ scattered several tiny villages.   (is, are)
4. Two thirds of our students _____ on to college.   (goes, go)
5. The scout troop _____ its annual camp-out tomorrow.   (begins, begin)
6. The panel sometimes _____ their ideas among themselves.   (discusses, discuss)
7. The main point of discussion now _____ wages.   (is, are)
8. There _____ never been any disagreement between the twins.   (has, have)
9. *Star Wars* _____ the first movie in the trilogy.   (was, were)
10. The team _____ putting on their uniforms.   (is, are)

23.1 Agreement With Confusing Subjects
• Practice 2

Exercise 1 **Making Confusing Subjects Agree With Their Verbs.** Underline the item in the parentheses that agrees with the subject of each sentence.

1. *The Wings of a Dove* (is, are) an acclaimed novel.

2. Everybody in the bank (was, were) stunned by the incident.

3. Marauding ants (was, were) one reason we left the picnic.

4. Behind the house (stands, stand) an old oak tree.

5. Six feet (is, are) the amount of wire we need.

6. Several of the hostages (was, were) released.

7. Above our heads (is, are) a skylight.

8. The squadron (was, were) flying off in various directions.

9. The committee (disagree, disagrees) on a course of action.

10. The news of his death (was, were) a surprise to everyone.

11. (There's, There are) only two roads leading to their house.

12. Mathematics (is, are) not one of my best subjects.

13. One cause of lung cancer (is, are) cigarettes.

14. Some of the ice cream (has, have) melted.

15. Several of the contestants (were, was) quite nervous.

16. The pliers (is, are) in the toolbox.

17. Half of my problems (was, were) solved by his generosity.

18. *North by Northwest* (is, are) a film I have seen three times.

19. The man's ethics (is, are) beyond reproach.

20. Twenty-five cents (is, are) more than enough for this.

Writing Application **Applying the Rules of Subject and Verb Agreement.** Use each item at the beginning of a sentence, followed by the verb *is* or the verb *are*.

1. either you or he

2. politics

3. some of the books

4. lumber and nails

5. behind the chair

6. fifty cents

7. confetti

8. most of the punch

9. both puppies

10. one of the games

1. _____

2. _____

3. _____

4. _____

5. _____

6. _____

7. _____

8. _____

9. _____

10. _____

23.2 Agreement Between Personal Pronouns and Antecedents • Practice 1

Agreement Between Personal Pronouns and Antecedents   A personal pronoun must agree with its antecedent in number, person, and gender. Use a singular personal pronoun with two or more singular antecedents joined by *or* or *nor*. Use a plural personal pronoun with two or more antecedents joined by *and*. Use a plural personal pronoun if any part of a compound antecedent joined by *or* or *nor* is plural. When dealing with pronoun-antecedent agreement, take care not to shift either person or gender. When gender is not specified, use *his or her* or rewrite the sentence.

PRONOUN-ANTECEDENT AGREEMENT

Jason got an A on *his* science report.

The lamppost has flowers around *it*.

Amy or Louise will lend you *her* notes.

Mom and Dad have left for *their* vacation.

Neither the attendants nor the bride showed *their* nervousness.

Every student must pay *his or her* own way.

All students must pay *their* own way.

▶ **Exercise 1**   **Choosing Personal Pronouns to Agree with Antecedents.**   Assume that each item below is an antecedent for a personal pronoun. After each, write *his, her, its,* or *their* to show which pronoun you would use to refer to it.

EXAMPLE: the general or an aide _____*his*_____

1. most teachers _____
2. the sports car _____
3. either Tom or Peter _____
4. Sally, Jane, or Carol _____
5. only one actress _____

6. Damian or Justin _____
7. each Cub Scout _____
8. several proposals _____
9. the new library _____
10. the best female vocalist _____

▶ **Exercise 2**   **Pronoun-Antecedent Agreement in Sentences.**   Write an appropriate personal pronoun to complete each sentence.

EXAMPLE: My sister and I clean _____*our*_____ own rooms.

1. Despite Tom's hard work, _____ probably will not win a prize.
2. We planted a lot of spinach this year, but no one will eat _____
3. Neither Beth nor Elena can find _____ history notes.
4. The lawyer and her clerk changed _____ line of defense.
5. Papa Walter thinks _____ garden is the best in the neighborhood.
6. Lionel offered to lend us _____ car.
7. All contestants must include _____ phone numbers on the form.
8. Vera, are these _____ gloves?
9. Janet has been studying all week for _____ driver's test.
10. Surely Bill and Kevin will give us _____ expert advice.

Name _____ Date _____

 23.2 # Agreement Between Personal Pronouns
and Antecedents • Practice 2

▶ **Exercise 1**   **Making Personal Pronouns Agree with Their Antecedents.**   Write an appropriate
personal pronoun to complete each sentence.

1. My aunt and uncle expressed _____ gratitude for the gift.

2. Neither my sisters nor Sue brought _____ books.

3. Every nation has _____ own distinctive culture.

4. Medical students should take _____ education seriously.

5. Did she have any trouble on _____ trip?

6. Mr. Gray and _____ associate will represent us.

7. Neither Karen nor Linda has handed in _____ paper.

8. Laura and Alyssa are working hard on _____ project.

9. We bought the car even though _____ tires were bald.

10. Neither Bob nor David has finished _____ education.

▶ **Exercise 2**   **Avoiding Shifts in Person and Gender.**   Underline the correct pronoun in
parentheses to complete each sentence.

1. Henry is studying French because (you, he) will need it in France.

2. We know that a good education is necessary if (we, you) are to get ahead in the world.

3. Typical of my friends and me is (our, their) generosity.

4. If people are amoral, society will impose restrictions on (your, their) freedom.

5. Venice is very appealing to tourists because of its canals and (her, its) great museums.

6. We all make mistakes, but (you, we) should try not to make the same mistake twice.

7. After people have worked long and hard, (they, you) need time for relaxation.

8. Many women are finding out that (you, they) can compete successfully with men in sports.

9. Let's not fill ourselves on the first course of the meal because (you, we) will be served four more
    courses.

10. Since that nation has not clearly defined its foreign policy, (she, it) has created distress abroad.

23.2 Agreement With Indefinite and Reflexive Pronouns • Practice 1

Agreement with Indefinite Pronouns   Use a singular personal pronoun when the antecedent is a singular indefinite pronoun. Use a plural personal pronoun when the antecedent is a plural indefinite pronoun. With an indefinite pronoun that can be either singular or plural, agreement depends on the antecedent of the indefinite pronoun.

AGREEMENT WITH INDEFINITE PRONOUNS
Neither of the boys would admit *his* mistake.
Several of the students handed in *their* reports early.
Most of the lawn has dandelions covering *it*. (lawn = singular antecedent)
Most of my friends take *their* education seriously. (friends = plural antecedent)

Agreement with Reflexive Pronouns   A reflexive pronoun must agree with an antecedent that is clearly stated.

REFLEXIVE PRONOUN AGREEMENT	
Incorrect	**Correct**
The trouble between Alex and *myself* began over a silly misunderstanding.	The trouble between Alex and *me* began over a silly misunderstanding.

▶ **Exercise 1**   **Making Personal Pronouns Agree with Indefinite Pronouns.**   Write an appropriate personal pronoun to complete each sentence.

EXAMPLE: Each of the girls studies at _____*her*_____ own desk.

1. Some of the hot dogs already have mustard on _____.

2. Some of the punch is not cold and needs ice cubes in _____

3. Few of the students have finished _____ rough drafts yet.

4. Everyone on the girls' hockey team provides _____ own uniform.

5. No one from the women's caucus would give _____ endorsement to the bill.

6. Several of the swimmers will exhibit _____ skills.

7. Much of the food had too much garlic in _____.

8. Has anyone from the men's club proposed _____ own plan?

9. All of the candidates spoke _____ minds during the debate.

10. I think some of these cookies have nuts in _____.

▶ **Exercise 2**   **Using Reflexive Pronouns Correctly.**   Underline the misused reflexive pronoun in each sentence. Write the correct pronoun on the line.

EXAMPLE: What is the trouble between Gina and himself ? _____*him*_____

1. Maxine and herself will meet us at the library. _____

2. No one but yourself would have been so thoughtful. _____

3. Phil and myself enjoy sailing. _____

4. Keith knew the secret, but he wouldn't even tell yourself. _____

5. Aunt Betsy asked you and myself to come for dinner. _____

Name _____ Date _____

 23.2 **Agreement With Indefinite and Reflexive Pronouns • Practice 2**

▶ **Exercise 1** **Making Personal Pronouns Agree With Indefinite Pronouns.** Underline the correct pronoun in each sentence.

1. Each of the candles shed (its, their) light into the room.
2. Before anyone joins this sorority, (she, they) must have an outstanding academic record.
3. All of the boys brought (his, their) books.
4. One of the linebackers has raised (his, their) hand.
5. Few of the teachers were willing to give up (his, their) Saturday mornings.
6. Either of the mules will carry (its, their) load without protesting.
7. All of the players have cleaned (his, their) uniforms.
8. Some of the meat had lost (its, their) tenderness.
9. Two of my sisters want (her, their) allowances increased.
10. Most of the campers have set up (his, their) tents.
11. Neither of my aunts gave me (their, her) support.
12. Each of the mobiles can be hung from (its, their) wire.
13. Somebody in the girls' gym left (her, their) locker open.
14. Some of the crew members wore (his, their) own helmets.
15. Neither of the women brought (her, their) husband.

▶ **Exercise 2** **Using Reflexive Pronouns Correctly.** Rewrite each sentence, correcting the misused reflexive pronoun.

1. Rachel and myself are the only ones taking the exam.

_____

2. The house was painted and furnished by ourselves.

_____

3. You should give yourself and myself a rest about now.

_____

4. Who but yourself would have remembered my birthday?

_____

5. Dad would take care of you, but only herself is here.

_____

▶ **Writing Application** **Making Pronouns and Antecedents Agree.** Write a sentence for each item below, using each as the antecedent of a personal pronoun.

EXAMPLE: both _____ *Both of the boys lost their jackets on the outing to the park.* _____

1. each _____
2. Neither Robert nor Douglas _____
3. actor _____
4. diamond _____
5. flight attendant _____

© Prentice-Hall, Inc.

23.3 Special Problems: Vague Pronoun Reference • Practice 1

Vague Pronoun References   A pronoun requires an antecedent that is either clearly stated or clearly understood. The pronouns *which, this, that,* and *these* should not be used to refer to a vague or overly general idea. The pronouns *it, they* and *you* should not be used with vague antecedents. Note that the use of *it* as a subject in such expressions as *It is raining* and *It is true* is acceptable and need not be avoided.

Vague Reference	Correct
Marlow had lost his job, and his girl had married his best friend. *This* is not what was upsetting him, though.	Marlow had lost his job, and his girl had married his best friend. *These two misfortunes* were not what was upsetting him, though.
In the *Farmer's Almanac,* it says that we are in for a long, cold winter.	The *Farmer's Almanac* predicts that we are in for a long, cold winter.
In the Midwest, *they* pronounce *Mary* and *marry* exactly alike.	*Midwesterners* pronounce *Mary* and *marry* exactly alike.

▶ **Exercise 1**   **Correcting Vague Reference Problems.**   Rewrite each sentence below to correct a vague reference involving *which, this, that,* or *these.*

EXAMPLE: The team lost two players and two games. That was mostly bad luck.

   The team lost two players and two games. All of the losses were mostly bad luck.

1. Cinderella had to stay home since she had no clothes for the ball. This did not seem fair at all.

   _____

2. The movie had lots of flashbacks and dream sequences. These confused me.

   _____

3. Nick got up early and washed the dishes. That startled me.

   _____

4. Mr. House makes the chalk squeak on the board, which I can't stand.

   _____

5. Wesley nodded sagely and jotted something in this notebook, but this didn't fool anyone.

   _____

▶ **Exercise 2**   **Solving More Problems With Pronoun Reference.**   Rewrite each sentence below that is faulty because of vague pronoun reference. If a sentence is correct, write *correct.*

EXAMPLE: It was after six o'clock when we arrived.

   correct

1. At the Middle School, they have an Olympic-size swimming pool.

   _____

2. In table tennis, you change servers with each five points that are scored.

   _____

3. In England, they call a freight car a "goods van."

   _____

4. It is now exactly three forty-five.

   _____

5. It says in the paper that schools will be closed on Election Day.

   _____

23.3 Special Problems: Vague Pronoun Reference • Practice 2

Exercise 1 **Correcting Vague Pronoun References.** Rewrite the sentences below, correcting the vague pronouns.

EXAMPLE: In our class, you must pay attention.

_____*In our class, we must pay attention.*_____

1. The juggler used ten balls in his act. That wasn't easy.

_____

2. In Mexico you must be a citizen to own oceanside property.

_____

3. A small child can easily choke on hard candy, which parents must be careful to prevent.

_____

4. Auto emissions must be reduced. A new law will ensure it.

_____

5. You can't buy tickets until the box office opens.

_____

6. Jason exaggerates the truth, and this makes me skeptical of his stories.

_____

7. The Grays serve clams at their banquets, which not everyone likes.

_____

8. Many poets use obscure symbols, and this confuses readers.

_____

9. Kay thinks she can't be hurt. This leads her to take risks.

_____

10. From where my cousin lives, you can see the ocean.

_____

Exercise 2 **Correcting Vague Pronoun References.** The following paragraph contains five vague pronoun references. On the lines below, rewrite the incorrect examples, correcting the vague pronoun references.

EXAMPLE: (vague) I worked at an ice-cream shop last vacation and enjoyed it very much.

(revised) _____*I worked at an ice-cream shop last vacation and enjoyed the job very much.*_____

    The first horses in America were brought by Spaniards. They soon attracted the interest of Indians. Seeing the speed and power that a horse gave its rider, they were determined to have them for their own. The Indians obtained many horses through trading with the Spaniards, but many others were stolen. They conducted raids on the herds of the Spaniards and those of other tribes. During these, some horses got away and formed herds of their own.

1. _____
2. _____
3. _____
4. _____
5. _____

23.3 Special Problems: Ambiguous or Distant Pronoun Reference Agreement • Practice 1

Ambiguous Pronoun References   A pronoun should never refer to more than one antecedent. The pronoun should always be tied to a single, obvious antecedent.

Ambiguous Reference	Clear Reference
Steve told Jesse that he might lose his job.	Steve told Jesse that Jesse might lose his job.

Avoiding Distant Pronoun References   A personal pronoun should always be close enough to its antecedent to prevent confusion.

Distant Reference	Corrected
Tire tracks from a dirt bike had furrowed the trail. The hikers exchanged glances and shook their heads. *They* seemed so out of place in the deep forest.	Tire tracks from a dirt bike had furrowed the trail. The hikers exchanged glances and shook their heads. *The tracks* seemed so out of place in the deep forest.

▶ **Exercise 1**   **Recognizing Problems of Pronoun Reference.**   In the spaces at the right, write the antecedent of each underlined pronoun. If the pronoun has no single antecedent to which it clearly refers, write *FR* (for faulty reference) in the space.

EXAMPLE: Betsy told Nancy her backhand was improving. ____*FR*____

1. Before leaving Mitzi with Grandma, we should tell her where we're going. _____

2. Ms. Loren explained to Michelle the passages she had just read. _____

3. The garden had been his uncle's hobby. A thick layer of mulch had separated each carefully tended bed of roses from the next. Now it was weedy and overgrown. _____

4. Volunteers fought the fire bravely, but they could only slow its steady advance. _____

5. After Nick told his father about the new job, he wished him luck. _____

▶ **Exercise 2**   **Correcting Problems of Pronoun Reference.**   On the lines below, rewrite four sentences in Exercise 1 which you labeled FR for faulty reference.

EXAMPLE: *Betsy told Nancy that Nancy's backhand was improving.*

1. _____
   _____

2. _____
   _____

3. _____
   _____

4. _____
   _____

23.3 Special Problems: Ambiguous or Distant Pronoun Reference Agreement • Practice 2

▶ **Exercise 1** **Correcting Ambiguous Pronoun References.** For the following sentences, underline the ambiguous pronoun references and, in the blank, write a correction.

EXAMPLE: When Jon asked his father if he could borrow the car, <u>he</u> said he needed it to go to work.
_____*Jon*_____

1. I looked for the article in the magazine, but I did not find it. _____

2. Andrea told Mimi that she was being given a promotion. _____

3. When my uncle takes my little brother to the park, he is very happy. _____

4. The Grays were supposed to send us some shells when they returned from their trip, but they haven't arrived yet. _____

5. When the child carried a stuffed rabbit with a big, fluffy tail onto the elevator, the door slammed shut upon it. _____

6. When the gypsy looked into her crystal ball for a picture of the future, it seemed hazy. _____

7. Both the problem and the solution are complicated. It requires concentration, so let's go through it again. _____

8. When Mark told his math teacher that he was moving to Iowa, he said he would miss him very much. _____

9. I gave Sean a shirt and tie for his birthday, but it did not please him. _____

10. Although the pool water and the air are chilly, it will become warmer as the day progresses. _____

▶ **Exercise 2** **Correcting Distant Pronoun References.** In the following sentences, underline the distant pronoun references and, in the blank, write a correction.

1. Several crumbling steps led down to the cellar. The walls had once been lined with the delicate wines from his vineyard. Arturo wondered whether they could support him. _____

2. At the helm stood the captain, gazing at the horizon as waves lapped softly at the ship's sides. Stealthily, the pirate crept aboard. He shouted to alert the crew. _____

3. Pieces of bleached driftwood lay undisturbed by the few people who came to wander on the sandy beach. They were twisted into fantastic shapes. _____

4. Hank plodded along behind the plow, muttering to himself about the newfangled machinery his neighbor had purchased. Well, he thought, it had done the job for him and his family in the past and would do so now. _____

5. Mary sat enshrouded in plastic. Like a porcupine prepared to defend itself, the beautician's mouth was spiked with bobby pins with which she mercilessly jabbed the scalp. Insensitive fingers twisted the wet strands of hair tightly around metallic spools. Gritting her teeth, she repressed a sudden urge to slap her assailant. _____

Degrees of Comparison • Practice 1

Recognizing Degrees of Comparison Most adjectives and adverbs have three different forms to show degrees of comparison.

DEGREES OF COMPARISON			
	Positive	**Comparative**	**Superlative**
Adjectives	safe dangerous ill	safer more dangerous worse	safest most dangerous worst
Adverbs	hard carefully badly	harder more carefully worse	hardest most carefully worst

Regular Forms Use -er or more to form the comparative degree and -est or most to form the superlative degree of most one- or two-syllable modifiers. Use more and most to form the comparative and superlative degrees of all modifiers with three or more syllables.

REGULAR FORMS OF COMPARISON			
One- and two-syllable modifiers	long homely thankful	longer homelier more thankful	longest homeliest most thankful
Three or more syllables	emotional awkwardly	more emotional more awkwardly	most emotional most awkwardly

▶ **Exercise 1** **Recognizing Degrees of Comparison.** Identify the degree of comparison of the underlined word in each sentence by writing *pos.* (positive), *comp.* (comparative), or *sup.* (superlative).

EXAMPLE: Harry may find it <u>harder</u> to succeed than William. *comp.*

1. There have been <u>fewer</u> cases of flu this year than last. _____
2. Melissa brought home an <u>excellent</u> report card. _____
3. This is the <u>coldest</u> September I can remember. _____
4. Gooden will surely be named <u>most valuable</u> player. _____
5. Jane will be <u>more cautious</u> on her next camping trip. _____
6. Kevin has the <u>hottest</u> bat in the league. _____
7. Harvey attacked his meal <u>greedily</u>. _____
8. Last night I had the <u>strangest</u> dream. _____
9. The patient seemed <u>more alert</u> after the medication had worn off. _____
10. Elmer began his speech <u>nervously</u>. _____

▶ **Exercise 2** **Comparing Adjectives and Adverbs.** Write the missing forms of each modifier.

EXAMPLE: friendly _____*friendlier*_____ _____*friendliest*_____

1. fanciful _____ _____
2. _____ _____ calmest
3. _____ more oddly _____
4. coarse _____ _____
5. angrily _____ _____

24.1 Degrees of Comparison • Practice 2

▷ Exercise 1 **Recognizing Positive, Comparative, and Superlative Degrees.** Identify the degree of each underlined modifier.

EXAMPLE: The problem was <u>more difficult</u> than I expected. ___*comparative*___

1. Their furniture is <u>more ornate</u> than mine. _____

2. Ursula is the <u>most artistic</u> person in her family. _____

3. I work <u>worse</u> under pressure. _____

4. She responded to the treatment <u>more quickly</u> than he. _____

5. The <u>wisest</u> policy is to wait until we know all our choices. _____

6. His philosophy is <u>difficult</u> to understand. _____

7. Jamie's talent for persuasion is <u>irresistible</u>. _____

8. Your foot will feel <u>better</u> if you walk on it. _____

9. She is the candidate's <u>most eager</u> supporter. _____

10. The new student did <u>badly</u> on the aptitude test. _____

▷ Exercise 2 **Forming Regular Comparative and Superlative Degrees.** Write the comparative and superlative form of each modifier.

EXAMPLE: light ___*lighter*___ ___*lightest*___

1. quick _____ _____

2. soon _____ _____

3. big _____ _____

4. helpless _____ _____

5. noble _____ _____

6. irritating _____ _____

7. tersely _____ _____

8. handsome _____ _____

9. difficult _____ _____

10. talkative _____ _____

11. arduous _____ _____

12. deadly _____ _____

13. clearly _____ _____

14. easy _____ _____

15. punctual _____ _____

16. virtuously _____ _____

17. fair _____ _____

18. red _____ _____

19. thirsty _____ _____

20. diligent _____ _____

Degrees of Comparison (Irregular Forms)
• Practice 1

Irregular Forms   The irregular comparative and superlative forms of certain adjectives and adverbs must be memorized.

IRREGULAR MODIFIERS		
Positive	**Comparative**	**Superlative**
bad	worse	worst
badly	worse	worst
far (distance)	farther	farthest
far (extent)	further	furthest
good	better	best
ill	worse	worst
late	later	last or latest
little (amount)	less	least
many	more	most
much	more	most
well	better	best

▶ **Exercise 1**   **Forming Irregular Comparative and Superlative Degrees.**   Write the appropriate form of the modifier in parentheses to complete each sentence.

EXAMPLE: The stew tastes _____*better*_____ since you added the mushrooms. (good)

1. Performers usually do _____ against strong competition than against weak. (well)

2. We could have walked _____ if Cal hadn't been with us. (far)

3. No one felt _____ than Tom about the misunderstanding. (bad)

4. Andy showed _____ interest of all in the weaving exhibit. (little)

5. Ours was the _____ plane to leave before the airport was fogged in. (late)

6. Your basic plan sounds good, but you need to develop it _____. (far)

7. Which place has the _____ pizza in town? (good)

8. That rise in his fever suggests that Jay might be getting _____. (ill)

9. Of all the children in the kindergarten, Jen behaves _____. (badly)

10. Next time we will try to see _____ exhibits than we did today. (many)

▶ **Exercise 2**   **Using Adjectives and Adverbs to Make Comparisons.**   Use each modifier in a sentence of your own to show a clear comparison. Use five comparative forms and five superlatives.

EXAMPLE: (much) _____*Didn't Phil eat more cake than I did?*_____

1. (bad) _____

2. (badly) _____

3. (well) _____

4. (many) _____

5. (good) _____

6. (ill) _____

7. (late) _____

8. (far) (distance) _____

9. (much) _____

10. (little) (amount) _____

24.1 Degrees of Comparison (Irregular Forms)
• Practice 2

▶ **Exercise 1** **Forming Irregular Comparative and Superlative Degrees.** Write the appropriate form of the underlined modifier to complete each sentence.

EXAMPLE: This restaurant is good, but that one is _____better_____ .

1. Carol did badly on the test, but Sue did even _____ .

2. I was late for practice, but Jim was even _____ .

3. Mother still feels ill, but yesterday she felt _____ .

4. Marty looks good in red, but he looks _____ in blue.

5. Evelyn lives farther from school than Ray, but Craig lives the _____ of the three.

6. I have little interest in math and even _____ physics.

7. My English teacher assigns more homework than my math teacher, but my history teacher assigns the _____ .

8. We drove quite far yesterday, but we must drive _____ today.

9. There was much commotion outside, but inside there was even _____ .

10. Jan has a better record than Lester, but Kerry has the _____ record of the three.

▶ **Writing Application** **Using Adjectives and Adverbs to Make Comparisons.** Write a sentence with each word in the degree indicated.

1. private—comparative

   _____

2. little (amount)—superlative

   _____

3. humble—positive

   _____

4. sudden—comparative

   _____

5. slowly—superlative

   _____

6. likely—superlative

   _____

7. much—comparative

   _____

8. badly—positive

   _____

9. bad—comparative

   _____

10. good—positive

   _____

24.2 **Clear Comparisons • Practice 1**

Using Comparative and Superlative Degrees Use the comparative degree to compare two people, places, or things. Use the superlative degree to compare three or more people, places, or things.

Comparative (comparing two)	Superlative (comparing three or more)
Ben stayed *later* than the others.	Ben stayed *latest* of all the guests.
Jack had a *better* answer than Steve.	Jack had the *best* answer in the class.
Part II was *more difficult* than Part III.	Part II was the *most difficult* section of the test.

▶ **Exercise 1** Using the Comparative and Superlative Degrees Correctly. Underline the correct form in each sentence.

EXAMPLE: I wish I had read the directions (more, most) carefully.

1. Paul will find the (less, least) excuse not to practice the piano.

2. Grandpa Hill is the (older, oldest) person I know.

3. We will examine the question (more, most) thoroughly next time we meet.

4. Antarctica is the (colder, coldest) place on earth.

5. The defense attorney then questioned the witness (more, most) closely.

6. Max is the (more, most) inquisitive child I have ever met.

7. Mr. Salvin will explain the experiment (more, most) fully tomorrow.

8. Paul has made the (fewer, fewest) errors of any player on the team.

9. The runner is trying to beat his own (faster, fastest) time.

10. Of all the movies in town, I am (more, most) eager to see the comedy.

▶ **Exercise 2** Using the Comparative and Superlative Degrees in Sentences. Use each of the following modifiers in two sentences, first in the comparative degree and then in the superlative degree.

EXAMPLE: (silly) *The clown on the right is sillier.*
                        The clown in the middle is the silliest.

1. (happy) _____
_____

2. (old) _____
_____

3. (tall) _____
_____

4. (friendly) _____
_____

5. (late) _____
_____

24.2 Clear Comparisons • Practice 2

▶ Exercise 1 **Using the Comparative and Superlative Forms Correctly.** Underline the correct comparative or superlative form in each sentence.

1. Gina's most recent babysitting experience was far (worse, worst) than the one before.
2. Kenny is the (more, most) interesting person at the party.
3. Greg is (funnier, funniest) than his brother Mark.
4. She is the (younger, youngest) person to win the award.
5. Which of the two cities is (farther, farthest) from here?
6. The book is (less, least) suspenseful now that I know the ending.
7. Moira is (better, best) at acting than her sister.
8. I was (more, most) embarrassed than he was.
9. Were you the (stronger, strongest) member of the team?
10. Which of the twins dances (better, best)?

▶ Exercise 2 **Supplying the Comparative and Superlative Degrees.** Write the appropriate comparative or superlative degree of the modifier in parentheses.

EXAMPLE: Linda is the ____fastest____ runner in our school. (fast)

1. It is much _____ today than it was yesterday. (warm)
2. Of the three sisters, Jill is the _____. (generous)
3. Todd is _____ than his brother. (tall)
4. This book is _____ than the last one I read. (long)
5. Thelma is _____ than I am. (graceful)
6. I am feeling _____ this morning than I did last night. (ill)
7. Which is _____, the gazelle or the jaguar? (swift)
8. Grandfather is the _____ person in town. (old)
9. Theresa writes _____ than I do. (well)
10. Of the ten speeches, the _____ one was given by Marilyn. (good)
11. Boston is _____ from New York City than Philadelphia is. (far)
12. There is _____ work to be done today than there was yesterday. (much)
13. Gwendolyn is _____ in math than she is in English. (good)
14. Louis is _____ than his brother. (clever)
15. This stamp is the _____ in my father's collection. (valuable)
16. That steak was the _____ I have ever seen. (good)
17. Which is your _____ arm? (strong)
18. Javaid speaks Urdu _____ than I ever will. (fluently)
19. I thought *Yentl* was the _____ of the two films we saw. (good)
20. Beatrice is the _____ person I have ever known. (lazy)

24.2 # Logical Comparisons • **Practice 1**

Logical Comparisons   Make sure that your sentences compare only items of a similar kind.

Unbalanced Comparisons	Correct
This year's team looks stronger than *last year*.	This year's team looks stronger than last year's.
The plants in Rita's den are lusher than her *kitchen*.	The plants in Rita's den are lusher than *those* in her kitchen.

When comparing one of a group with the rest of the group, use the word *other* or the word *else*.

Illogical	Correct
Our school has a *better* team *than any school* in town.	Our school has a *better* team than any *other school* in town.

▶ **Exercise 1**   **Making Balanced Comparisons.**   Rewrite each sentence, correcting the comparison.

EXAMPLE: Al's bike is newer than Len.

_____ *Al's bike is newer than Len's.* _____

1. Joe's artistic ability is greater than Andrew.

   _____

2. Lana's SAT scores were higher than her twin sister.

   _____

3. Today's temperature is higher than yesterday.

   _____

4. The instructions for baking a cake are easier than petit fours.

   _____

5. Fran's lunch had fewer calories than Donna.

   _____

▶ **Exercise 2**   **Using *Other* and *Else* in Comparisons.**   Rewrite each sentence, correcting the comparison.

EXAMPLE: Donna can swim farther than anyone on the team.

_____ *Donna can swim farther than anyone else on the team.* _____

1. My sister handles pressure better than any member of our family.

   _____

2. Ted's workout schedule is more strenuous than any player's on the team.

   _____

3. Julie worked harder than anyone on the decorating committee.

   _____

4. The park on Woodcut Lane is more beautiful than any in town.

   _____

5. My new kitten is more playful than any kitten.

   _____

24.2 # Logical Comparisons • **Practice 2**

▶ **Exercise 1** **Making Balanced Comparisons.** Rewrite each sentence, correcting the unbalanced comparision.

EXAMPLE: Mona's speech was more interesting than Luke.

Mona's speech was more interesting than Luke's.

1. The bill of a duck is broader and flatter than a chicken.

   _____

2. Aunt Mary's homemade jam is sweeter than Aunt Helen.

   _____

3. The mileage we get on this car is better than that car.

   _____

4. A stroll in the park is less invigorating than the beach.

   _____

5. The grade on Tim's paper is better than Jeff's paper.

   _____

6. The horn of a rhino is more valuable to poachers than an elephant.

   _____

7. Replacing the roof with slate tiles will be more expensive than shingles.

   _____

8. Today's weather is warmer than yesterday.

   _____

9. The dog was sidetracked because the scent of the deer was stronger than the rabbit.

   _____

10. These directions for assembling a radio are less complicated than a tricycle.

   _____

▶ **Exercise 2** **Using** *Other* **and** *Else* **in Comparisons.** Rewrite each sentence, correcting the illogical comparison.

EXAMPLE: Chicago is larger than any city in Illinois.

Chicago is larger than any other city in Illinois.

1. This cereal is more nutritious than any brand.

   _____

2. Her explanation of photosynthesis is simpler than anyone's.

   _____

3. Our neighbor is a better carpenter than anyone in town.

   _____

4. She reads more mystery stories than anyone I know.

   _____

5. Seneca Lake is deeper than any of the Finger Lakes.

   _____

24.2 Clear Comparisons (Absolute Modifiers)
• Practice 1

Absolute Modifiers Avoid using absolute modifiers illogically in comparisons.

Illogical	Correct
That painter has the *most unique* style of any contemporary artist.	That painter's style is *unique* among contemporary artists.
	That painter has the most *unusual* style of any contemporary artist.
His answer was *more final* than we expected.	His answer was *final*.
	His answer was *firmer* than we expected.

▶ **Exercise 1**   **Correcting Illogical Comparisons.**   Rewrite each sentence, correcting any illogical comparisons.

EXAMPLE: Of all the children, Janet looks most identical to her mother.

_____ *Of all the children, Janet looks most like her mother.* _____

1. The accident was less fatal than it might have been.

_____

2. Now that he is in the first grade, Pat draws rounder circles than he once did.

_____

3. He threw the ball straighter than an arrow.

_____

4. I have never seen a deader plant than that fern.

_____

5. The challenger's position is more opposite mine than the incumbent's.

_____

▶ **Exercise 2**   **Writing Clear Comparisons.**   For each of the following items, write an effective comparison in one sentence.

EXAMPLE: Compare two animals that are household pets.

_____ *Dogs are usually more obedient than cats.* _____

1. Compare two of your favorite actors.

_____

2. Compare three of your favorite desserts.

_____

3. Compare one school subject to another.

_____

4. Compare the difference in calories among three fruits.

_____

5. Compare one after-school job with another.

_____

24.2 Clear Comparisons (Absolute Modifiers)
• Practice 2

▶ Exercise 1 **Avoiding Absolute Modifiers in Comparisons.** Rewrite each sentence, correcting the illogical comparison of an absolute modifier.

1. This coin is the most unique one in my collection.

_____

2. The tarantula's bite was less fatal than we expected.

_____

3. After the hike he was more entirely exhausted than I was.

_____

4. Her second novel was more perfect than her first.

_____

5. The court will announce its most final decision today.

_____

6. The names of the most final contestants were announced.

_____

7. Of the five puppies, Sparky is most identical to the sire.

_____

8. This will be our most final chance to win the race.

_____

9. By revising my essay, I made it more perfect.

_____

10. His hairstyle is more unique than hers.

_____

▶ Writing Application **Writing Effective Comparisons.** Use the following instructions to write five sentences of your own.

1. Compare your own taste in clothing with a friend's.

_____

2. Compare one country's form of government with another country's form of government.

_____

3. Compare English with another language.

_____

4. Compare three of your favorite movies.

_____

5. Compare achievements of two different athletes.

_____

25.1 Negative Sentences • Practice 1

Recognizing Double Negatives Do not write sentences with double negatives.

CORRECTING DOUBLE NEGATIVES	
Double Negatives	**Corrections**
Erin *can't* have *no* dairy foods.	Erin *can't* have any dairy foods.
	Erin can have *no* dairy foods.
We *won't never* finish in time.	We *won't* ever finish in time.
	We will *never* finish in time.
Nobody told us *nothing* about it.	*Nobody* told us anything about it.
	They told us *nothing* about it.

► Exercise 1 **Recognizing Double Negatives.** Label each sentence below as *DN* (containing a double negative) or C (correct).

EXAMPLE: I'll never let nobody else know the secret. _____*DN*_____

1. The detective said nothing about her suspicions. _____
2. Mandy will never let nobody help her. _____
3. You won't never find a more loyal friend than Jason. _____
4. The library will no longer be open on Friday evenings. _____
5. After next week, we won't have no more classes. _____
6. There wasn't nobody home when we got there. _____
7. The police haven't a single clue in the case. _____
8. You shouldn't have no more trouble with the car now. _____
9. Neither of those boys don't know the way to the park. _____
10. We can never ask no questions during a test. _____
11. I can't find nothing good to eat in the house. _____
12. No one is allowed to give us no help with the project. _____
13. No one could do anything to stop Dave from leaving the party. _____
14. There weren't any seats nowhere in the stadium. _____
15. There has been no sign of activity in the house for a week. _____
16. Barbie couldn't get nobody to take her to the dance. _____
17. Rick didn't get no homework done last night. _____
18. Nothing has changed since Alice left school. _____
19. Donnie would not leave until the concert was over. _____
20. There aren't no dishes left to be washed. _____

► Exercise 2 **Correcting Double Negatives.** Rewrite correctly five of the sentences you labeled *DN* in Exercise 1.

EXAMPLE: _____*I'll never let anybody else know the secret.*_____

1. _____
2. _____
3. _____
4. _____
5. _____

25.1 # Negative Sentences • Practice 2

▶ **Exercise 1** **Avoiding Double Negatives.** Underline the word in parentheses that makes each
sentence negative without forming a double negative.

1. I don't want to hear (none, any) of your excuses.

2. Never ask (anybody, nobody) for money.

3. Martin (was, wasn't) nowhere near the vase when it fell.

4. We can't buy (no, any) material without more money.

5. Without a passport no one (can't, can) cross the border.

6. The store will not make (no, any) more deliveries today.

7. The detective (could, couldn't) find no evidence.

8. I didn't come because I (didn't, did) have my car.

9. You had better not go (anywhere, nowhere) in this weather.

10. Frozen meat shouldn't (never, ever) be refrozen.

11. We don't need (any, no) more apples.

12. Carol didn't see (anybody, nobody) else at the bus stop.

13. Micah (was, wasn't) invited to neither of the parties being thrown that night.

14. Patrick can't do (no, any) more work tonight.

15. You shouldn't (never, ever) bite off more than you can chew.

16. I didn't want to be (anywhere, nowhere) near that place.

17. Sheila (could, couldn't) see no reason to leave her hometown.

18. We (can, can't) go nowhere with an empty gas tank.

19. Nobody said (anything, nothing) for a full minute.

20. The Palmerson family (is, isn't) planning no more garage sales this year.

▶ **Exercise 2** **Correcting Double Negatives.** The following paragraph contains ten double
negatives. Correctly rewrite each sentence that contains a double negative so that each double negative
is eliminated.
EXAMPLE: Our neighbor didn't want no more pets. ___*Our neighbor didn't want any more pets.*___
    Curtis had never been to no circus before. One reason was that no circus had never come to his town.
Another reason was that he never had no extra money. If a circus had been at a nearby town, he wouldn't
have been able to take no train to see it. Recently, however, all that changed. Curtis's family is poor no
longer. They wouldn't be missing no circus this year. "I don't want none of my children to stay home this
weekend," said Curtis's dad. "Don't let nothing interfere with our plans this Saturday. We won't be wearing
no old clothes, either. Maybe I couldn't buy you no new jackets last year, but this year is different. We don't
have to worry no longer."

1. _____

2. _____

3. _____

4. _____

5. _____

6. _____

7. _____

8. _____

9. _____

10. _____

25.1 Forming Negative Sentences Correctly
• Practice 1

Forming Negative Sentences Correctly   Use only one negative word in a single clause. Do not use *but* in its negative sense with another negative. Do not use *barely, hardly,* or *scarcely* with another negative.

Double Negatives	Correct Negative Sentences
I can't believe that you *haven't never* seen that movie.	I can't believe that you have *never* seen that movie.
You *haven't but* one minute left.	You *haven't* more than a minute left.
	You have *but* one minute left.
I can *hardly never* win an argument with Bruce.	I can *hardly* ever win an argument with Bruce.

Understatement   Understatement can be achieved by using a negative word and a word with a negative prefix.

UNDERSTATEMENTS
After the indictment, the cabinet member's resignation was *not unexpected.*
Although we were not enthusiastic, *no one* was *unwilling* to help with the project.

▶ **Exercise 1**   **Avoiding Problems With Negatives.**   Underline the word or words in parentheses that make each sentence negative without creating a double negative.

EXAMPLE: I (could, couldn't) hardly keep from laughing.

1. There weren't (but, more than) a dozen people at the meeting.
2. The neighbors couldn't believe that we didn't hear (anything, nothing).
3. We (had, hadn't) barely enough food to go around.
4. Pete (always, never) eats but half a sandwich for lunch.
5. You shouldn't have told the caller that there (was, wasn't) nobody home.
6. The patient has shown (any, no) recurring symptoms.
7. Aunt Ellie didn't stay (but, more than) a few minutes.
8. Jared hardly (ever, never) gets anywhere on time.
9. Elaine didn't see (any, no) animals on the nature hike.
10. We couldn't find (anywhere, nowhere) else to sit.

▶ **Exercise 2**   **Using Understatement.**   Rewrite each sentence, using understatement.

EXAMPLE: The news was expected.

     The news was not unexpected.

1. The chore was possible, but difficult.

   _____

2. My parents were pleased with my grades.

   _____

3. Mr. Dow's comments were inspiring.

   _____

4. The campaign speech was emotional in its appeal.

   _____

5. Though not beautiful, the child is appealing.

   _____

25.1 **Forming Negative Sentences Correctly**
• Practice 2

▶ **Exercise 1** **Avoiding Problems With Negatives.** Underline the word in parentheses that makes each sentence negative without creating a double negative.

1. There (was, wasn't) but a single apple left.

2. John (is, isn't) scarcely listening to me.

3. There (wasn't, was) anything special about the program.

4. We couldn't find (nobody, anybody) who would help.

5. Cindy (was, wasn't) barely recognizable in her new dress.

6. I (haven't, have) taken no aspirin for my headache.

7. You shouldn't buy (none, any) of the produce here.

8. I've never traveled (anywhere, nowhere).

9. Diane (couldn't, could) hardly remember me.

10. Don't let (anyone, no one) in on our secret.

▶ **Exercise 2** **Correcting Double Negatives.** Rewrite each sentence, correcting the double negative.

1. Brad didn't like none of our suggestions.

_____

2. We weren't scarcely out to sea when the storm started.

_____

3. Wanda would not agree to give us no money.

_____

4. Fred doesn't want but ten minutes of your time.

_____

5. We couldn't hardly understand what the waiter was saying.

_____

6. There isn't no way I can finish my report on time.

_____

7. Mr. Walker doesn't want no late papers.

_____

8. I couldn't call you because I hadn't but a nickel.

_____

9. Sam hadn't scarcely begun mowing when it rained.

_____

10. The children didn't want no nap this afternoon.

_____

25.2 # Common Usage Problems • Practice 1

Solving Usage Problems Study the items in the usage glossary in your textbook, paying particular attention to similar meanings and spellings, words that should never be used, pairs that are often misused, and problems with verb forms.

TYPES OF PROBLEMS		
Similar Spellings	all together, altogether	beside, besides
Wrong Words	irregardless	these here
Misused Pairs	emigrate, immigrate	healthy, healthful
Verb Forms	emigrate, immigrate	must of *for* must have

▶ **Exercise 1** **Avoiding Common Usage Problems.** Underline the word or words in parentheses that correctly complete each sentence.

EXAMPLE: The twins are quite different (from, than) each other.

1. If he (don't, doesn't) finish his chores soon, we'll be late for the movie.

2. Ellis Island was the first stop for many people (emigrating, immigrating) to the United States.

3. (Beside, Besides) the regular menu, the restaurant offers daily specials.

4. The whole audience (burst, busted) out laughing.

5. Please (bring, take) this note to the office on your way out.

6. Few of the students were (enthused, enthusiastic) about the schedule.

7. Once the plans were made, we were (anxious, eager) to start our trip.

8. Can we (adapt, adopt) that city's plan to fit our small town?

9. The library is just a short (way, ways) past the post office.

10. Grandma (learned, taught) me all she knew about cooking.

▶ **Exercise 2** **Correcting Common Usage Problems.** Underline the word or expression that creates a usage problem in each sentence below. Then correctly rewrite each sentence, using formal English.

EXAMPLE: Less people attended the parade this year than last.
    Fewer people attended the parade this year than last.

1. The police accused that the suspect could be placed at the scene.

   _____

2. We had ought to have been more careful.

   _____

3. Ali has decided that being accepted at a good school is her principle goal.

   _____

4. Sean missed the field trip due to the fact that he was ill.

   _____

5. Everyone agreed that Paula had offered real good arguments.

   _____

25.2 Common Usage Problems • Practice 2

▶ **Exercise 1** **Avoiding Usage Problems.** Underline the correct expression to complete each sentence.

1. (Advice, Advise) me as you think best.

2. The patient (accuses, alleges) malpractice by the surgeon.

3. (A lot, Alot) of us felt we had been robbed of our rights.

4. Carol was adversely (affected, effected) by the new law.

5. He refuses to (accept, except) his limitations.

6. I lost the necklace (somewhere, somewheres) in the theater.

7. (Every one, Everyone) of the pigeons wanted to be fed.

8. Does anyone know where the fuse box (is, is at)?

9. A sign was strung (among, between) the two posts.

10. Your tuxedo is (all together, altogether) inappropriate.

11. I was (awfully, very) sorry to learn of his illness.

12. (Beside, Besides) swollen glands, I also had a sore throat.

13. We selected milk (being as, since) it had calcium.

14. The reason Al is so knowledgeable about other countries is (because, that) his Dad always took him everywhere.

15. I jogged (a while, awhile) before dusk.

16. We (done, have done) everything possible to help them.

17. I submitted an outline of the (exam, examination).

18. White bread (doesn't, don't) have much nutritional value.

19. The three boys strengthened (each other's, one another's) determination with encouraging words.

20. Report immediately to Ms. Edwards in our (ad, advertising) department.

▶ **Exercise 2** **Avoiding Usage Problems.** Underline the correct expressions to complete each sentence.

1. Our new car uses (fewer, less) gasoline than our old one.

2. Rita (gone, has gone) to the movies twice this week.

3. Both his bicycle and his skateboard were broken. The (former, latter) had a flat tire.

4. (Colorful, Lovely) flowers grew in profusion on the hill.

5. You can (climb, get) to the tree house by using the rope.

6. The patient's pulse was beating (slow, slowly).

7. (Except for, Outside of) Amy and Carol, no one came to the barbecue.

8. Snow was a strange (phenomena, phenomenon) in New Orleans.

9. The boys (seen, had seen) the ballet twice before.

10. The print media (carry, carries) more advertising than television does.

Capitalization • Practice 1

Capitals for First Words   Use capital letters to begin words in each situation shown in the chart.

CAPITALS FOR FIRST WORDS	
Complete Sentences	Have you told your parents about your grade?
Quoted Sentences	The guard ordered, "Admit no one after 6 P.M."
Sentences After Colons	His plight is desperate: He is starving.
Interjections	Oh! Now look what you've done.
The Words *I* and *O*	To thee, O England, I pledge my life.
Lines of Poetry	Tell me where is fancy bred, Or in the heart or in the head?—William Shakespeare

Capitals for Proper Nouns   Capitalize each important word in all proper nouns, as shown below.

CAPITALS FOR PROPER NOUNS	
People/Animals: Emma Lazarus, Lassie	*Geographical Names:* Main Street
Specific Events: the Civil War	*Specific Places:* Hammer Field
Religious Terms: the Old Testament	*Specific Groups:* House of Commons
Specific Vehicles: the Titanic	*Brand Names:* Kleenex

Capitals for Proper Adjectives   Capitalize most proper adjectives.

With Capitals	Without Capitals
Proper Nouns as Adjectives: Indian festival	*Common Terms:* india ink
Brand Names: Quaker oatmeal	*Most Prefixes:* pro-British press
Combinations: Arab—Israeli tension	*Compounds:* French-speaking men

▶ **Exercise 1**   **Using Capitals for First Words.**   Underline the word or words that should be capitalized in each sentence.

EXAMPLE: <u>unfortunately</u>, <u>i</u> didn't hear the teacher say, "<u>you</u> may begin."

1. the poem begins, "when i was one and twenty."

2. yes, we should get something for Ms. Hall. what do you have in mind?

3. goodness! you must know i didn't mean that.

4. the coach asked, "why didn't you go after that first pitch?"

5. she was very happy: she had done very well on her first test.

▶ **Exercise 2**   **Capitalizing Proper Nouns and Proper Adjectives.**   Underline each word or word part that should be capitalized in the sentences below.

1. Mr. wilson usually buys foreign cars, but his new car is a studebaker.

2. While in the middle east, the carrolls visited many new testament shrines.

3. Our new neighbors come from cairo, egypt, but were educated in england.

4. During their cruise on the *viking maiden*, the hills stopped in jamaica.

5. There are several spanish-speaking students at amity high school.

26 # Capitalization • Practice 2

▶ **Exercise 1**   **Capitalizing First Words.**   Underline the word or words that should be capitalized in each sentence.

EXAMPLE: perhaps i made a mistake.

1. nonsense! what did Dr. Reston really expect?

2. the poet Alfred Lord Tennyson wrote, "o, hark, o, hear!"

3. i know exactly what he wanted: he wanted us to turn over all of our records to him.

4. edward Bulwer Lytton once wrote, "the easiest person to deceive is one's own self."

5. she reported about three kinds of ships: schooners, steamboats, and clipper ships.

6. abraham Lincoln said that the United States was "conceived in liberty."

7. drive carefully! the life you save may be your own.

8. "my new science teacher is terrific," said Maria. "i actually understand molecules."

9. did you buy this record yesterday? where?

10. "nature has given us two ears," said Henrietta Temple, "but only one month."

▶ **Exercise 2**   **Capitalizing Proper Nouns.**   Underline the word or words that should be capitalized in each sentence.

EXAMPLE: The george washington bridge stretches across the hudson river between new york and new jersey.

1. The ithaca high school thespians will perform on april 18 and 19.

2. In europe the first outbreak of the black plague occurred in 1346.

3. The four daughters of the greek god zeus were athena, hebe, artemis, and aphrodite.

4. They lived on mount olympus with eight other olympians.

5. The republican party and the democratic party plan to hold separate rallies at the capitol building in washington, d.c.

6. Our family hopes to vacation on waikiki beach at either christmas or easter.

7. Of the faculty members, only angela watkins could speak fluently in five languages: english, french, german, polish, and russian.

8. When we studied the bible, we compared the old testament with the new testament.

9. I can always spot the moon, but I have trouble with the milky way and the big dipper.

10. Mary o'hara wrote to the university of maryland and to georgetown university for college bulletins.

▶ **Exercise 3**   **More Work With Proper Nouns.**   Underline the word or words that should be capitalized in each sentence. Some sentences might not need further capitalization.

EXAMPLE: A pulitzer prize was awarded to david b. davis.

1. The papers of w. h. auden are housed at the new york public library.

2. Our teacher asked for a description of the rivers, mountains, and deserts in that area of the country.

3. My father wants to see the john f. kennedy center for the performing arts and the smithsonian institution.

4. The middle ages lasted almost a thousand years, from 476 to 1450.

5. Denmark, located on the jutland peninsula, has a beautiful cosmopolitan capital.

26 # Capitalization in Titles and Letters
• Practice 1

Capitals for Titles   Capitalize titles of people and titles of works.

People	Works
Social: the Earl of Sandwich	*Book:* Pinocchio
Business: Supervisor Cosgrove	*Periodical:* TV Review
Military: Captain Jenkins	*Poem:* "Paul Revere's Ride"
Government: Ambassador Margaret Howe	*Story:* "The Boat"
Religious: Sister Anne	*Painting:* Mona Lisa
Compound: Chief Justice Burger	*Music:* Waltz of the Flowers
Abbreviations: Dr., Sr., M.D.	*Courses:* Personal Typing II

Capitals in Letters   Capitalize the first word and all nouns in letter salutations and the first word in letter closings.

Salutations	Closings
My dear Amanda,	With deep affection,
Dear Senator Jacobs:	Sincerely yours,

▶ **Exercise 1**   **Using Capitals in Titles.**   Underline the words that should be capitalized in the sentence.

EXAMPLE: Our class play will be *kind hearts and coronets*.

1. Didn't corporal Vargo just get a promotion?

2. "Mending wall" is one of Frost's most famous poems.

3. Will attorney general Adamson prosecute the case herself?

4. Tomorrow James Lawlor, sr., will discuss the new tax bill.

5. The song "I could have danced all night" is from the musical *my fair lady*.

6. Governor and mrs. Kerwin hosted a reception for general Hargrove.

7. The famous orient express ran between Paris and Istanbul.

8. Parts of the book *in cold blood* appeared in a literary magazine.

9. The text of reverend Jacobson's sermon was taken from genesis.

10. Roberta Necome, r.n., will lead the baby-sitting classes.

▶ **Exercise 2**   **Using Capitals for Salutations and Closings.**   Rewrite each of the following letter parts, adding the missing capitals.

EXAMPLE: dear aunt eloise, _____*Dear Aunt Eloise,*_____

1. dear captain vargo, _____

2. your loving cousin, _____

3. with gratitude, _____

4. my dear friend, _____

5. very truly yours, _____

6. dear father hartman, _____

7. yours always, _____

8. dear sir or madam: _____

9. my dearest george, _____

10. with warmest wishes, _____

26 # Capitalization in Titles and Letters
• Practice 2

▶ **Exercise 1** **Capitalizing Titles of People and Things.** Underline any words or abbreviations that should be capitalized in each sentence.

EXAMPLE: I have an appointment with Carl <u>hill</u>, <u>d.d.s.</u>, today.

1. Barbara W. Tuchman's highly regarded bestseller is entitled *a distant mirror: the calamitous 14th century.*

2. We will invite grandmother, aunt Lucy, and mr. McDowell.

3. The speaker, ex-senator Morton, entertained the audience.

4. At the seminar professor Riley speculated on the place that former secretary of state Dulles will occupy in history.

5. I gave my cousin a subscription to the magazine *sports unlimited.*

6. I repeat, mayor Grant, you have not answered my question.

7. William O. Douglas, long a member of the Supreme Court, never became chief justice.

8. We explained our concerns to governor-elect O'Hara.

9. One of Edna St. Vincent Millay's best sonnets is "on hearing a symphony of Beethoven."

10. Commander in chief Reagan appeared with his wife.

▶ **Exercise 2** **Capitalizing Parts of a Letter.** Underline any words or abbreviations that should be capitalized in the following letter.

461 carol drive
joliet, illinois 60435
October 12, 1986

mr. alan ternes, editor
natural history
american museum of natural history
central park west at 79th street
new york, new york 10024

dear mr. ternes:

   i understand why the writer of the article in natural history magazine found fishing enthusiasts upset by the large numbers of carp in north american waters. any fish that changes the environment of lakes and rivers so that popular game fish will no longer thrive there upsets me too!
   however, carp also live in waters where game fish cannot survive. therefore, i am glad that the united states fish and wildlife service and others have been unsuccessful in getting rid of the carp. perhaps, in the future, hardy, adaptable carp may be appreciated here, as they are already in europe and asia.

                    sincerely yours,
                    nancy hansler

27.1 End Marks • Practice 1

Basic Uses of End Marks   Use a period to end a declarative sentence, a mild imperative, and an indirect question. Use a question mark to end an interrogative sentence, an incomplete question, or a statement intended as a question. Use an exclamation mark to end an exclamatory sentence, a forceful imperative sentence, or an interjection expressing strong emotion.

Periods	Question Marks	Exclamation Marks
The rain has stopped.	Will it rain tomorrow?	What a storm that was!
Check your work.	When?	Run for your life!
I wonder who it is.	That's an *s*?	Yeah! We won!

Other Uses of End Marks   Use a period to end most abbreviations and after numbers and letters in outlines. Use a question mark in parentheses (?) after a fact or statistic to show its uncertainty.

Periods	Question Marks
Fran Pringle, M.F.A.	We have a $150 (?) deductible.
I. English Loan Words	May 12 (?) will be Mother's
A. Native American Words	Day this year.

▶ **Exercise 1**   **Using End Marks for Sentences and Phrases.**   Write the proper end mark at the end of each item.

EXAMPLE: There must be some mistake. It costs that much ____?____.

1. How beautiful those flowers smell _____

2. Which teams are playing on Saturday _____

3. Sue asked how we had made the gingerbread houses _____

4. The score is tied. Hooray _____

5. Stop immediately _____

6. Damian is not here yet _____

7. What a surprise their visit was _____

8. Mom wondered how many people would actually come _____

9. Be careful riding your bike after dark _____

10. How long will that film be playing _____

▶ **Exercise 2**   **Using End Marks in Your Own Sentences.**   Follow the directions to write your own sentences.

EXAMPLE: Write a sentence that suggests uncertainty about a date.
          She will turn eighteen on October 15(?).

1. Write a sentence that shows uncertainty about an amount.

   _____

2. Write a sentence that begins with a strong interjection.

   _____

3. Write an indirect question.

   _____

4. Write a forceful imperative sentence.

   _____

5. Write a statement intended as a question.

   _____

⬤27.1 **End Marks • Practice 2**

▷ **Exercise 1**   **Using End Marks.**   Write the proper end mark or end marks for each item.

EXAMPLE: The stream sparkled as it flowed over the rocks ____ . ____

1. To whom did you give the award for citizenship _____
2. Our basketball team just won an incredible victory _____
3. Watch out _____ This road is full of dangerous
   curves _____
4. Lisa asked when the next dance performance is scheduled _____
5. How can we tell which pair of sneakers is better _____
6. You divided your report into three sections _____
   Why _____
7. Wonderful _____ Did you expect to win _____
8. The fish has tiny bones in it _____ Chew it carefully _____
9. What makes the Marx Brothers still so funny _____
10. The Narragansett Indians were clustered in what is now Washington County, Rhode
    Island _____

▷ **Exercise 2**   **Using Periods and Question Marks in Other Situations.**   Rewrite each item that needs one or more periods, adding them where necessary. If an item does not require any change, write *correct*.

EXAMPLE: This package is for Mary Low, MD.
   ____*This package is for Mary Low, M.D.*____

1.
I Fly fishing _____
   A Tackle _____
        1 Rod _____
        2 Reel _____
        3 Lures _____

2. The recipe listed the following: 2 oz of melted cheese and 2 tsp of vegetable oil.
   _____

3. Must you always watch TV after dinner?
   _____

4. The roar of the SST is deafening.
   _____

5. Dr Johnson's office hours begin at 2:00 PM.
   _____

27.2 Commas (Compound Sentences, Series, Adjectives) • Practice 1

Commas With Compound Sentences   Use a comma before the conjunction to separate two independent clauses in a compound sentence.

COMPOUND SENTENCES
We had hoped to get an early start, but Angie overslept. Hal spent all day shopping, yet he bought only one pair of socks.

Commas With Series and Adjectives   Use commas to separate three or more words, phrases, or clauses in a series. Use commas to separate adjectives of equal rank, but not to separate adjectives that must stay in a specific order.

With Commas	Without Commas
I went to the movies with Beth, Ann, and Susan. They live in a huge, sprawling mansion.	I went to the movies with Beth and Susan. They live in a sprawling brick mansion.

▶ **Exercise 1**   **Using Commas Correctly.**   Add commas where they are needed. Not all sentences need commas.

EXAMPLE: The basic ingredients for the dough are butter flour and salt.
           The basic ingredients for the dough are butter, flour, and salt.

1. The walkers maintained a brisk steady pace.

2. Lauren can not afford the tuition so she is applying for financial aid.

3. Ali ordered soup broiled fish and a salad.

4. Several boisterous hecklers interrupted the speech.

5. The cake was trimmed with tiny chocolate curls.

6. I had hoped to see Linda but she wasn't at the party.

7. Hemlock wreaths pine branches and clumps of holly decked the huge foyer.

8. Few things are worse than tough overcooked meat.

9. Grandma received a bouquet of beautiful yellow roses.

10. Please drop these letters at the post office and then you can go to the library.

▶ **Exercise 2**   **Recognizing Rules for Commas.**   Describe the comma rule for each sentence in Exercise 1 by writing *compound sentence, series, equal adjectives,* or *adjectives in order.*

EXAMPLE: *series*

1. _____

2. _____

3. _____

4. _____

5. _____

6. _____

7. _____

8. _____

9. _____

10. _____

27.2 # Commas (Compound Sentences, Series, Adjectives) • Practice 2

▶ **Exercise 1** **Using Commas to Separate Independent Clauses.** Add commas where they are needed.

EXAMPLE: I wanted to go to the concert but it was sold out.
I wanted to go to the concert, but it was sold out.

1. The poor tarantula could not move fast for it had only seven instead of eight legs.
2. Ted wants to study this morning but he plans to jog first.
3. Can you reach a decision now or do you need more time?
4. We plan to visit Greece and Turkey and then we hope to explore Israel and Egypt.
5. I love to bake cakes but my specialty is apple pie.
6. Born in London in 1757, the poet William Blake never attended school for few Londoners of that time had any formal education.
7. My brother is a student of the Bible so he is familiar with both the Old and the New Testament.
8. Lisa listens only to jazz but Sally prefers rock music.
9. We can get the information we need for our report from the library or we can visit the museum exhibit next week.
10. My uncle will either fly or he will take the train.

▶ **Exercise 2** **Punctuating Simple Sentences and Compound Sentences.** Add commas where they are needed. Not every sentence needs commas.

EXAMPLE: I have not seen the movie but I hope to see it soon.
I have not seen the movie, but I hope to see it soon.

1. My sister plans to take several business courses and then open her own record shop.
2. The high school baseball season ends in early June and football practice begins in late July.
3. This magazine is published weekly but that one is published only once a month.
4. Aspirin can occasionally cause intestinal bleeding but other drugs can also have dangerous side effects.
5. Most new fuel-efficient cars have four-cylinder engines and offer a choice of manual or automatic transmission.
6. A home safe is useful but irreplaceable papers should be kept in a bank vault.
7. The car swerved sharply to the right and crashed into the picket fence.
8. Gold was discovered in California early in 1848 but the first news of the discovery was not published until March.
9. I have always loved outdoor sports and often play tennis and softball.
10. I don't care for most of the recent war movies nor did I care for some of the earlier ones.

27.2 # Commas (Introductory Material, Parenthetical and Nonessential Expressions) • Practice 1

Commas After Introductory Material

INTRODUCTORY MATERIAL
Introductory Word: Honestly, I don't know how it happened.
Introductory Phrase: Even after having seen the movie twice, I still get scared.
Introductory Clause: When the bell rang at the end of the period, I was surprised.

Commas With Parenthetical and Nonessential Expressions   Use commas to set off parenthetical and nonessential expressions.

PARENTHETICAL EXPRESSIONS	
Direct Address:	I am sure, Harry, that you will win.
Certain Adverbs:	It is clear, therefore, that we must act soon.
Common Expressions:	Marcia, on the other hand, is quite shy.
Contrasting Expressions:	That notebook is mine, not Jake's.

Essential Expressions	Nonessential Expressions
My uncle James Forest lives in Ohio.	James Forest, my uncle, lives in Ohio.
The teacher talking to the principal is Mme. Duval.	Mme. Duval, now talking to the principal, is my French teacher.
The man who lives next to us was born in Warsaw.	Mr. Walenski, who lives next to us, was born in Warsaw.

> **Exercise 1** **Recognizing Introductory Material.** Write the introductory word, phrase, or clause in each sentence, and add the needed comma.

EXAMPLE: No I haven't seen Shelley today. _____No,_____

1. Actually I haven't finished the book yet. _____

2. Without a moment's hesitation Tim agreed. _____

3. Looking slightly confused Mary checked the map. _____

4. Although they liked the idea they weren't willing to help. _____

5. Happily no one was injured. _____

6. Before we started out we checked the gas gauge. _____

7. When Jed asked me to help I couldn't refuse. _____

8. Bert would you like to join us? _____

9. To get good seats we should leave early. _____

10. Of course we could always walk home. _____

> **Exercise 2** **Using Commas With Parenthetical and Nonessential Expressions.** Add commas where they are needed. One sentence needs no commas.

EXAMPLE: The price tag should read $9.95 not $19.95.
           The price tag should read $9.95, not $19.95.

1. The lead article an exposé on hiring practices created a furor.

2. Peter should be here any minute I am sure.

3. A player who goes out of turn is automatically eliminated.

4. His paper is missing the footnotes not the bibliography.

5. We have been reading *Beowulf* the oldest epic poem in English.

27.2 Commas (Introductory Material, Parenthetical and Nonessential Expressions) • Practice 2

▶ **Exercise 1** **Using Commas After Introductory Material.**   Insert commas where they are needed. If a sentence does not require a comma, write *correct*.

EXAMPLE: Chris have you finished the assignment yet?
Chris, have you finished the assignment yet?

1. Oh do you really believe that? _____

2. In front of the long column of troops on the field the general introduced his successor. _____

3. If you were to offer her another opportunity do you think she would accept your invitation? _____

4. Since you are interested in muckrakers I suggest you read books by Lincoln Steffens or Ida Tarbell. _____

5. Chosen by secret ballot Professor Watkins immediately took charge of the committee. _____

6. Walking slowly and breathing heavily the campers finally straggled into town. _____

7. Without much hope the detectives searched the entire building. _____

8. While traveling Europe Lord Byron began to write a long poem. _____

9. Carefully the doctor prescribed the proper antibiotics for the illness. _____

10. After years of no regulation of business the Fair Labor Standards Act of 1938 set minimum ages for employment. _____

▶ **Exercise 2** **Using Commas to Set Off Parenthetical Expressions.**   Insert commas to set off parenthetical expressions in the following sentences.

EXAMPLE: His reasoning therefore was faulty.
His reasoning, therefore, was faulty.

1. His record I suppose should be a factor in the case.

2. I simply do not agree you realize with your argument.

3. Another consideration should be her years of experience however.

4. Who is your favorite actor Bill?

5. She tried in fact to contact the owner several times.

6. The hostility of the group she believes will soon be overcome.

7. Do you want both the name and the address of each student Ms. Jones?

8. We played racquetball not tennis.

9. You must therefore arrive on time.

10. I must however admit that I was surprised.

27.2 Commas (Other Uses) • Practice 1

Other Uses of the Comma   When a date, a geographical name, or an address is made up of two or more parts, use a comma after each item except in the case of a month followed by a day. Use commas to set off a title following a name. Also use commas in the other situations shown in the chart below.

Dates	June 6, 1944, was D-Day.
Geographical Names	Boise, Idaho, is her hometown.
Addresses	Send your entries to Town Hall, 1352 Main Street, Branford, Connecticut 06405
Names With Titles	Martin Barber, S.T.D., will preach on Sunday.
Salutations and Closings	Dear Mrs. Cox, Sincerely yours,
Large Numbers	1,798 envelopes 2,867,321 people
Elliptical Sentences	Tom is studying French; Sue, German.
Direct Quotations	"You're kidding," Jill said.
To Prevent Confusion	Next to John, Bob is my best friend.

▶ **Exercise 1**   **Adding Commas to Sentences.**   Insert commas where they are needed.

EXAMPLE: Edwin Marshall D.Ed. will become the new superintendent.
Edwin Marshall, D.Ed., will become the new superintendent.

1. The vacant lot next to 521 Main Street Essex New Hampshire will be the site of the new condominium office complex.

2. Mom's gift is an angora sweater; Dad's leather gloves.

3. The magazine's paid circulation is 1278394 subscribers.

4. Alison wondered aloud "How many people will we have room for?"

5. Philip Bancroft M.D. is reported to be on the brink of a major discovery.

6. For his mother Jason had prepared a special surprise.

7. Cornwallis's surrender to Washington at Yorktown Virginia on October 19 1781 ended the Revolutionary War.

8. The contractor estimated that the porch would cost $9750.

9. "Jared will join us" Angie said "if he can get off work early."

10. Together with Jeanne Marie will be in charge of decorations.

▶ **Exercise 2**   **Punctuating a Letter.**   Add commas wherever necessary in the following letter.

528 Prospect Street
Wilmington Delaware 19803
April 3 1985

Dear Steve

   We have been here since Friday March 30 and we are having a wonderful time. Together with David Sam and I went camping over the weekend near Elkton Maryland. It's been great.

   Before I left you had asked me for Ben's new address which I forgot to give you. It is as follows: Mr. Benjamin Marple 515 West Seymour Street Philadelphia Pennsylvania 19129.

   See you next week!

Your friend
Danny

27.2 # Commas (Other Uses) • Practice 2

▶ **Exercise 1** **Using Commas in Other Situations.** Insert commas where necessary in the following sentences.

EXAMPLE: The speed of light is 186000 miles per second.
The speed of light is 186,000 miles per second.

1. Rudyard Kipling was born in Bombay India on December 30 1865.

2. Paul Santini Jr. is in my Spanish class.

3. Lisa Sullivan D.D.S. has an office in Houston Texas.

4. The party on Friday February 6 was a huge success.

5. On June 12 1988 they will graduate.

6. Have you ever lived in Seattle Washington?

7. He is going to study in Paris France next year.

8. They camped in Calgary Alberta Canada last summer.

9. Smith Construction Company Inc. built the auditorium.

10. On May 1 1985 he began work as a landscaper; she as a dental hygienist.

▶ **Exercise 2** **Using Commas in Letters.** Insert commas where necessary in the following letter.

2304 South Street
Fort Lauderdale Florida 33316
December 18 1986

Dear Nat

I can tell from your last letter that your summer plans are all wrapped up. Your summer sounds terrific; mine questionable.

With high hopes I wrote to a number of summer travel camps to apply for a job as counselor. All but one have turned me down and I'm still waiting to hear from that one. I worry that maybe I got the address wrong. Maybe I wrote 182 Shady Lane Lawrenceville Vermont instead of 128 Shady Lane Lawrenceville Vermont. Maybe I got the ZIP code wrong and wrote 10663 instead of 01663. At least I've now memorized the page in the catalog (page 1423) where the address is found.

My parents are fond of telling me "Keep your chin up." Nevertheless I'm still getting a bit nervous.

Your friend
Jody

▶ **Exercise 3** **Using Commas Correctly.** Insert commas where necessary in each of the following sentences.

EXAMPLE: A surprise party I think is a good idea.
A surprise party, I think, is a good idea.

1. When I asked my father for advice he told me I was old enough to make my own decisions.

2. The five explorers traveling through the jungle in intense heat reached the bank of the river on Thursday June 5.

3. Reaching the platform Congressman Brooks the featured speaker waved to the crowd.

4. A monthly newsletter is published by the American Civil Liberties Union 22 East 40th Street New York NY 10016.

5. Alice will you please list the magazines newspapers and books in your bibliography?

27.3 Semicolons and Colons • Practice 1

The Semicolon Use semicolons in situations such as those illustrated in this chart.

USES OF THE SEMICOLON	
With Independent Clauses	Andy ordered a pizza; Bill wanted a hamburger.
With a Conjunctive Adverb	Audrey has a bad cold; consequently, she won't be able to play in the game tonight.
With a Transitional Expression	Jim is an excellent student; as a matter of fact, he is at the top of the class.
With Items That Already Have Commas	Tammy, who has always been active in student government, is running for class president; but it looks as if Jo may win.

The Colon Use a colon in situations such as those shown in the following chart.

SOME USES OF THE COLON	
Lists	All the garnishes on the platter were edible: carrot curls, radish roses, and parsley sprigs.
Quotations	The host raised his glass: "Happy holidays to all!"
Summary Sentences	The doctor prescribed a strict diet: Fats and salt were almost entirely prohibited.
Formal Appositives	We finally decided on the perfect choice: Brenda.
Numerals Giving Time	6:15 A.M. 9:25 P.M.
Periodical References	*Science Week* 28:182 (volume: page number)
Biblical References	Genesis 3:15 (chapter: verse)

▶ **Exercise 1** **Using Semicolons Correctly.** In the sentences below, commas are used where semicolons are needed. Circle these commas to show that semicolons are needed instead.

EXAMPLE: The group included Sam (,) an artist, Tim, a musician (,) and Stan, an actor.

1. Paul has studied piano for three years, he will give a recital soon.

2. Louise missed her bus, as a result, she will be quite late.

3. I enjoy fruit, cheese, or nuts, which are healthful snacks, but they will never replace pastries.

4. Martha greatly admires her older sister, she is a brain surgeon.

5. Jack's best sport is basketball, his brother excels at soccer.

▶ **Exercise 2** **Using Colons Correctly.** Add colons where they are needed.

EXAMPLE: The loudspeaker crackled "The 530 flight to New York is now boarding."
The loudspeaker crackled: "The 5:30 flight to New York is now boarding."

1. The doctor warned against high-cholesterol foods eggs, butter, and steak.

2. We have a choice of two trains the 810, a local, or the 825, an express.

3. The quotation in Act 4 II is from Psalms 117 22.

4. Alison paused "I wonder which way to turn."

5. There is only one candidate I can support Terry.

27.3 Semicolons and Colons • Practice 2

> **Exercise 1** **Understanding the Use of the Semicolon.** In each of the following sentences, insert semicolons where necessary. Some of the sentences may require only a comma to separate independent clauses.

EXAMPLE: We tried hard to win however, the Tigers beat us.
    We tried hard to win; however, the Tigers beat us.

1. I expected an important package this morning therefore, I waited several hours for the mail.

2. Sam, who lives near the library, has been assigned to do the research and Tom will organize the final report.

3. Prince Edward Island is in Canada's Eastern Maritimes British Columbia is on the West Coast.

4. My friends intended to go shopping but they were unable to get someone to drive them.

5. "Perhaps the most valuable result of all education is the ability to make yourself do the thing you have to do, when it ought to be done, whether you like it or not it is the first lesson that ought to be learned."—Thomas Huxley

6. Our hope was to coordinate our efforts accordingly, we waited several hours for instructions.

7. On April 24, 1800, an act of Congress established the Library of Congress two provisions of the act were for "the purchase of such books as may be necessary for the use of Congress" and for "fitting up a suitable apartment" to house the new volumes.

8. My sister plans to attend college next year in fact, she has already been accepted at one.

9. After the hurricane we surveyed the shoreline, which bore the brunt of the storm inland bungalows, without roofs and often a heap of rubble and local roads, strewn with debris and fallen trees.

10. My grandparents arrived early and my parents were somewhat embarrassed by the condition of our house.

> **Exercise 2** **Understanding the Use of the Colon.** In each of the following items, insert colons where necessary.

EXAMPLE: They gasped when they opened the gift a live turkey.
    They gasped when they opened the gift: a live turkey.

1. My aunt arrived at the airport at 10 17.

2. Danger This water is polluted.

3. Dear Senator Robinson

4. I want to repeat my point of view clearly We cannot permit a change in policy at this time.

5. At 2 30 in the afternoon, I arrived for my first job interview.

6. Sue Ellen intends to study several major composers Bach, Haydn, Mozart, Beethoven, Brahms, and Wagner.

7. A visit by the Queen of Sheba is described in First Kings 10 8.

8. The process is somewhat involved It requires three separates stages, each a month apart.

9. F. Scott Fitzgerald described brilliance in this way "The test of a first-rate intelligence is the ability to hold two opposed ideas in the mind at the same rate, and still retain the ability to function."

10. He excelled in one sport soccer.

27.4 Quotation Marks: Direct Quotations
• Practice 1

Quotation Marks for Direct Quotations A direct quotation represents a person's exact speech or thoughts and is enclosed in quotation marks (" "). An indirect quotation reports only general meaning and does not require quotation marks. In writing direct quotations, use a comma or colon after an introductory expression and a comma, question mark, or exclamation mark after a quotation followed by a concluding expression. If an expression falls in the middle of a quoted sentence, set it off with commas. If it falls between two quoted sentences, treat it as a concluding expression.

Direct Quotations	Indirect Quotations
Pete asked, "What time is the game?"	Pete asked what time the game was going to begin.
"What time is the game?" Pete asked.	
"It seems unlikely," Gail said, "that we will win."	Gail thought it was unlikely that we would win.
"Move fast!" Ted shouted. "That tree is about to fall on you."	Ted shouted to me to move fast because a tree was about to fall on me.

▶ **Exercise 1** **Distinguishing Between Direct and Indirect Quotations.** Label each sentence below *D* (for direct quotation) or *I* (for indirect quotation).

EXAMPLE: The teacher said, Take out a sheet of paper for a quiz.   _____D_____

1. Mrs. Potter asked me to watch little Jesse tomorrow afternoon. _____
2. Timmy stood on tiptoe: I know I can reach it. _____
3. Are the reports due on Friday or Monday? Pam inquired. _____
4. Dave thinks that he can get an extra ticket for the concert. _____
5. We need a little more ribbon, Paula observed, or maybe a piece of yarn would do. _____
6. That sweater looks like terrific on you, Nancy remarked. _____
7. Tom observed that membership has been dropping off lately. _____
8. I asked the clerk if she had the same size in a different color. _____
9. Oh! Jenny wailed. The meat is burned. _____
10. The manager reported that attendance so far had exceeded all expectations. _____

▶ **Exercise 2** **Using Quotation Marks Correctly.** In each sentence labeled *D* above, add quotation marks where they are needed. On the spaces provided below, rewrite each sentence labeled *I* so that it contains a direct quotation. Use quotation mark where they are needed.

EXAMPLE: _____The teacher said, "Take out a sheet of paper for a quiz."_____

_____

_____

_____

_____

_____

27.4 Quotation Marks: Direct Quotations
• Practice 2

▶ **Exercise 1** **Using Quotation Marks with Direct Quotations.** In the following sentences, add quotation marks where they are needed. The quoted fragment has been underlined so that you can tell where it begins and ends. If no additional punctuation is needed, write *correct*.

EXAMPLE: My father explained why he did not agree with me.   ___*correct*___

1. Please be home on time for your father's birthday dinner tonight, my mother reminded me. _____

2. If you have trouble understanding the chapter, said Miss Knopf, read it over a second time. _____

3. The guard insisted, You must have a pass before I can allow you to enter. _____

4. I found out that the show was sold out, she moaned, after I waited in line for two hours. _____

5. The policeman said that both lanes of the highway were temporarily closed. _____

6. Robert Frost wrote a poem about someone who stopped to watch the woods fill up with snow. _____

7. When I try to memorize a long speech, I said, I go through endless agony. _____

8. No, I'd prefer to visit Austria and Denmark this summer, Jim replied. That is why I am saving all of the money I can this winter. _____

9. The senator explained that he could not possibly support the highway construction bill. _____

10. About two miles down the road, you will see a cluster of three or four excellent restaurants, explained the travel guide.

11. The lecturer explained, The discovery of gold in California in 1849 brought to the west coast a huge rush of people. _____

12. The sailor said that one of the most fearsome displays of nature is a storm at sea. _____

13. The manatee, explained the biologist, has a flat, broad tail. _____

14. Lacrosse is my favorite game, said James, but it is not popular in this country. _____

15. If the flag is flying at night, it should be lighted, said Mrs. Fredericks.

▶ **Exercise 2** **Using Quotation Marks with Direct Quotations.** The following paragraphs contain ten direct quotations. Add quotation marks where they are needed.

Have you ever wondered how the Tournament of Roses parade began? asked Seymour.

In fact, replied Cecily, I have.

Seymour said, I was just reading about it. It is a very interesting story, and I'll be happy to tell you all about it. I'm listening, said Cecily.Seymour began by telling Cecily that there had been a terrible blizzard in New York City in 1888. This blizzard might have been the spark that set off the Tournament of Roses parade, he said. As heavy snow buried New York, he continued, the people of Pasadena saw an opportunity.

Cecily asked, What do you mean by that?

Well, replied Seymour, there were only a few thousand people in Pasadena at the time, and the city was eager to grow. They thought that using flowers as live decorations in the middle of winter would be attractive to easterners.

Did it work? asked Cecily.

Well, asked Seymour, do you have any idea how big Pasadena is today?

27.4 # Quotation Marks With Other Punctuation
• Practice 1

Other Punctuation Marks With Quotation Marks   Always place a comma or a period inside the final quotation mark. Always place a semicolon or colon outside the final quotation mark. Use the meaning of the whole sentence to determine the placement of question marks and exclamation marks.

PLACING OTHER PUNCTUATION MARKS	
Commas and Periods	"It is unlikely," Ed said, "that it will rain."
Colons and Semicolons	Len observed, "I think I can fix this bike"; then he explained the problem.
Question Marks and Exclamation Marks	Beth asked, "Will you be ready by 3:00?"
	Didn't Beth say, "You should be ready by 3:00"?

Quotation Marks in Special Situations   Use single quotation marks for a quotation within a quotation. Use three ellipsis marks in a quotation to show that words have been omitted. When writing dialogue, begin a new paragraph with each change of speaker. For quotations longer than a paragraph, put quotation marks at the beginning of each paragraph and at the end of the final paragraph.

SPECIAL SITUATIONS FOR QUOTATIONS	
Quotations Within Quotations	Mr. Salvin asked, "What poem begins, 'This is the forest primeval'?"
Omitted Words	The famous line "Not by bread alone . . . " appears in both Luke and Deuteronomy.
Dialogue	"Grades are certainly an important factor in college admissions. However, most colleges consider other factors as well.
	"In addition to academic achievements, colleges generally look for students who have a range of interests. Participation in sports and other school activities are definite assets," Ms. Banks said.
	"What about outside activities not related to school?" asked a student in the back row.

▶ **Exercise 1**   **Punctuating Direct Quotations.**   Add missing punctuation marks below.

EXAMPLE: Amy asked, Didn't Cole Porter write the song Night and Day?
        Amy asked, "Didn't Cole Porter write the song 'Night and Day'?"

1. Didn't Mom say, Be sure you're home by midnight?

2. Phil complained, This train is always late; just then it pulled in.

3. I hope, Janice said, that Kevin will be able to play tomorrow.

4. Do we have any soda or fruit juice? Len asked.

5. Mabel shrieked, Go for help immediately!

6. Anna began, It seems to me ...; then her voice trailed off.

7. Don't you agree, Paula asked, that we should try to help?

8. Who can tell me, Ms. Bailey asked, who wrote the poem Mending Wall?

9. The child mumbled, I'm stuffed; then he pushed his plate away.

10. Possibly, Norma suggested hopefully, a few more people will come.

▶ **Exercise 2**   **Paragraphing Dialogue.**   Write a short dialogue between you and a friend on the subject of college and career choices. Have one of the speakers go on for two paragraphs.

_____

_____

_____

_____

27.4 Quotation Marks With Other Punctuation
• Practice 2

Exercise 1   **Using Other Punctuation Marks with Quotation Marks.**   In each of the following sentences, add quotation marks. The quoted fragments are underlined.

EXAMPLE: How terrible it was when Jennifer announce, I must leave!
How terrible it was when Jennifer announced, "I must leave"!

1. Ask not what your country can do for you. Ask what you can do for your country.—John F. Kennedy
2. I'll be here Thursday, she cried, springing to the saddle. Good-bye. Quick, Ellen!—Emily Brontë
3. In the first sentence of George Orwell's *1984*, the clocks are <u>striking thirteen</u>.
4. The commander asked, Have all of the troops taken their positions?
5. I know what he expects, she sighed. If only I can reach those lofty goals.
6. Don't fire until you see the whites of their eyes!
7. Rose, my love! Cried Mrs. Maylie, rising hastily and bending over her. What is this? In tears! My dear child, what distresses you?—Charles Dickens
8. I accept his pledge of support; we need every volunteer we can get.
9. Did she say, I'd like to help?
10. Listen, I said to Raymond. You may be right.

Exercise 2   **Writing Original Dialogue.**   Write a few lines of original dialogue. Use two different characters and include a few lines of description. Enclose the lines of dialogue in quotation marks. Include enough conversation tags so that there will be no confusion about who is speaking.

_____

_____

_____

_____

_____

Exercise 3   **Using Ellipsis Marks and Single Quotation Marks.**   In each of the following sentences, insert double quotation marks (" ") and single quotation marks (' ') as needed.

EXAMPLE: I asked, Were you serious when you said, I won't?
I asked, "Were you serious when you said, 'I won't'?"

1. In a low voice, my sister whispered, Yes, and broke into a smile.
2. Wasn't it Richard Grafton who wrote, Thirty days hath September…, the poem that all children recite?
3. I remember the first line of my paper: "In 'The Adventure of the Speckled Band,' the lady in black greets the great detective with, It is fear, Mr. Holmes."
4. My favorite Dickinson poem is the one that begins, I'm Nobody! …
5. Part of the quote is … for happiness is the gift of friendship.
6. Again and again I asked, Please, please come; but in the end he refused.
7. One song from the musical *Showboat* ends with … then perhaps I might fall back on you.
8. Then I told Mother, Stone walls do not a prison make …, and I thought she would hit the roof.
9. Patrick Henry's speech of March 23, 1775, ended with … but as for me, give me liberty or give me death!
10. I wrote Shelley's famous line, O Wind, if Winter comes, can Spring be far behind? in my notebook.

27.4 # Quotation Marks and Underlining
• Practice 1

Underlining and Quotation Marks   Underline the titles of books, plays, periodicals, newspapers, long poems, movies, radio and TV series, long musical compositions, albums, and works of art. In addition, underline the names of individual land, air, sea, and space craft; foreign words not yet accepted into English; numbers, symbols, letters, and words used to name themselves; and words that you want to stress.

UNDERLINING	
Titles	**Other Uses**
<u>Great Expectations</u> (novel)	the <u>Twentieth Century Limited</u> (train)
<u>Under Milkwood</u> (play)	The <u>Viking Princess</u> (ship)
<u>Yellow Submarine</u> (movie)	The play was a <u>tour de force</u>. (foreign phrase)
<u>M.A.S.H.</u> (TV series)	That <u>i</u> looks like an <u>e</u>. (letters)
<u>Los Angeles Times</u> (newspaper)	You have misspelled <u>thief</u>. (word as word)
the <u>Mona Lisa</u> (painting)	That belongs to <u>me</u>. (stressed word)

Use quotation marks around the titles of short written works, episodes in a series, songs, and parts of long musical compositions or collections.

QUOTATION MARKS	
"The Open Boat" (short story)	"Tomorrow" from <u>Annie</u> (song)
"Annabel Lee" (poem)	"On Knowledge" from <u>The Prophet</u>
"Impromptu" (one-act play)	

Do not underline or place in quotation marks the names of sacred writings and their parts or the titles of government charters, alliances, treaties, acts, statutes, or reports.

EXAMPLE: the Torah, Acts of the Apostles (religious works)
        the Constitution, Kellogg-Briand Pact (government documents)

▶ **Exercise 1**   **Punctuating Different Types of Works.**   Use underlining or quotation marks with the works in each sentence. One item does not require punctuation.

EXAMPLE: The Cole Porter hit True Love is from the movie High Society.
        The Cole Porter hit "True Love" is from the movie <u>High Society</u>.

1. The first five books of the Old Testament are called the Pentateuch.

2. The first of the Canterbury Tales is The Knight's Tale.

3. The symbol & is used in the names of some businesses.

4. The newspaper Variety keeps theater folk au courant on their profession.

5. Andrea consistently misspelled sheik in her report on Saudi Arabia.

▶ **Exercise 2**   **More Work with Underlining and Quotation Marks.**   Follow the directions for Exercise 1. Again, one item does not require punctuation.

1. Mr. Dalbert sailed to Europe on the Queen Elizabeth 2 and returned on the Concorde.

2. Justine is the first of four parts in The Alexandria Quartet.

3. Most people enjoyed the movie Constitution this weekend.

4. We were asked to read the entire Constitution this weekend.

5. My favorite chapter in Tom Sawyer is The Glorious Whitewasher.

27.4 Quotation Marks and Underlining
• Practice 2

▶ **Exercise 1** **Recognizing the Many Uses of Underlining.** In each of the following sentences, underline where necessary.

1. They sailed for Europe on the Queen Elizabeth 2.

2. I used the book The Stranger to analyze the style of Camus.

3. She never crosses her t's or dots her i's.

4. Next season the repertory theater will perform the plays Richard III, All's Well that Ends Well, and Henry V.

5. Picasso's painting Guernica, once at the Museum of Modern Art, has been returned to the artist's native country.

▶ **Exercise 2** **Using Underling and Quotation Marks for Titles.** In each sentence, add underlining or quotation marks where needed. If neither is required, write *correct*.

1. Two of Emily Dickinson's best poems are I Like to See it Lap the Miles and I Heard a Fly Buzz—When I Died. _____

2. We discussed the St. Louis Chronicle newspaper in class. _____

3. The book Historic Sites in Pennsylvania will be useful in your survey. _____

4. My favorite song from the musical Brigadoon is The Heather on the Hill. _____

5. I was very impressed with the book The Sea Around Us by Rachel Carson. _____

▶ **Exercise 3** **Using Quotation Marks and Underlining.** In each of the following sentences, add quotation marks and underlining as needed.

1. I enjoyed Raisin in the Sun, a play by Lorraine Hansberry.

2. I wonder, she mused, whether my work will ever be done.

3. I own a print of Paul Cezanne's painting The Cardplayers.

4. Mary Martin starred in a number of Broadway shows including Peter Pan.

5. Will Rogers summed up Hoover's defeat by Roosevelt by stating, The little fellow felt that he never had a chance . . . .

6. A new edition of The World Almanac is published each year.

7. "Then my grandfather said, Forget him, and he never mentioned his name again."

8. I want to buy a CD album titled Jazz Classics.

9. The treaty will not be signed until all the troops are removed, said the majority leader.

10. Yes, she answered. We have agreed to meet with their representative tomorrow.

11. I stayed up all night reading Edna Ferber's book Saratoga Trunk.

12. My aunt asked, How do you plan to go from Seattle to San Francisco?

13. Chapter 8, The Logic Revolution, concludes with the War of Independence.

14. The full title of Richard Barber's book is The Arthurian Legends: An Illustrated Anthology.

15. I considered what you said, announced the principal, and decided to approve the plan.

Name _____ Date _____

 27.5 **Dashes • Practice 1**

Dashes Use dashes to indicate an abrupt change of thought, a dramatic interrupting idea, or a summary statement. Use dashes to set off a nonessential appositive, modifier, or parenthetical expression when it is long, when it is already punctuated, or when you want to be dramatic.

USES OF THE DASH	
Change of Thought	I'm almost finished—oh, no, someone's at the door.
Dramatic Interruption	Kevin's party—it's sure to be a huge, noisy one—is on Saturday night.
Summary Statement	La Maison, Chez Pierre, and L'Etoile—all are excellent French restaurants in town.
Nonessential Element	That red sweater—you know, the one with the reindeer knitted in—was a gift from my aunt.
	That bright object—you saw it too, didn't you?—may have been a UFO.

▶ **Exercise 1** **Using the Dash.** Add dashes where they are needed in the following sentences.

EXAMPLE: Judy's essay she wrote it in only half an hour won first prize.
　　　　　Judy's essay—she wrote it in only half an hour—won first prize.

1. That circus act the one with the aerialist walking a wire high above the ground always makes me uneasy.
2. The meeting didn't you say it was at Tom's house? begins at 8:00.
3. The players, the coaches, and the grounds crew all were given a bonus.
4. The new corporate president he worked his way up from stock boy, you know is sure to make some changes.
5. I hope that Ellen won't be oh, here she is now.
6. Our team is winning the game no, the other team just scored a touchdown.
7. Bruce Springsteen, Mick Jagger, Roger Daltry all are famous rock stars.
8. This Sunday's game it should be the best one this season starts at 1:00.
9. Morton Cooper he's a very gentle old man who loves to play chess is staying at our house.
10. Once this storm passes if it ever does the weather should be beautiful.

▶ **Exercise 2** **More Work With Dashes.** Follow the instructions for Exercise 1.

1. Rodgers and Hammerstein's works *Carousel, Oklahoma,* and *South Pacific* come immediately to mind are classics of the American musical theater.
2. Many consider *Long Day's Journey into Night* it is a largely autobiographical play to be Eugene O'Neill's greatest work.
3. Stephen Spielberg's new movie have you seen it yet? is sure to be a great success.
4. I can't find my ah, there they are.
5. Washington, Jefferson, Lincoln and Teddy Roosevelt these are the Presidents whose faces are carved in the granite of Mount Rushmore.

Name _____   Date _____

27.5 Dashes • Practice 2

27.5 Dashes • Practice 2

▶ **Exercise 1**   **Using the Dash.**   Add one or two dashes to each of the following sentences.

EXAMPLE: The vital measure of a newspaper is not its size but its spirit that is, its responsibility to report the news fully, accurately, and fairly.
   The vital measure of a newspaper is not its size but its spirit—that is, its responsibility to report the news fully, accurately, and fairly.

1. Computers have changed the world in countless ways have you seen our new school lab? most of them for the better, both in the short-run and in the long-run.

2. Old trunks filled with out-of-date clothes, projects abandoned years ago, scrapbooks, photo albums all of these we found hidden away as if forever in the attic of Aunt Lucy's house.

3. They wandered all day through the village a forgotten spot filled with thatched houses, horse mounts, and weather beaten signs.

4. Andrea has been working in the lab for weeks now oh, my, what was that noise?

5. Major disasters floods, hurricanes, tornadoes, and the like tend to bring out the best in some people and the worst in others.

6. Mr. Thomas who had studied for many years in Paris, Rome, and London now hoped to be able to make a living in the United States.

7. Their parties for example, the one where everyone had to bring a pet are known for their hilarity and occasionally for their lingering effect.

8. Before we can leave, we must check to make sure we have everything that do you realize I forgot to pick up the tickets?

9. His company he has worked there twenty years has recently decided to move across country, taking any employees who wish to relocate.

10. Our basketball team, our football team, our tennis team, and our soccer team all of them had a winning season this year.

▶ **Exercise 2**   **Using the Dash.**   Rewrite each of the following sentences by inserting, where appropriate, the remark in parentheses. Then, set off the remark by adding a dash or dashes to the sentence.

EXAMPLE: The huge house was painted pink. (And I do mean huge)
   The huge—and I do mean huge—house was painted pink.

1. The snow fell so heavily that the main highway was closed.   (Wait until you hear this!)

_____

2. Rowena met Adrian three times a year at the cottage by the sea.   (no more)

_____

3. What would you do if your mother were watching you?   (that sweet woman)

_____

4. In all her life, my grandmother never allowed her picture to be taken.   (ninety-two years)

_____

5. She claimed that the "mechanical box" was nothing compared to a portrait painter.   (the camera)

_____

162 • Grammar Exercise Workbook   © Prentice-Hall, Inc.

Name _____ Date _____

Parentheses Use parentheses to set off asides and explanations only when the material is not essential or when it consists of one or more sentences. Use parentheses to set off numbers or letters used with items in a series and with certain numerical references such as birth and death dates.

USES OF PARENTHESES	
Phrases	The old house (ugly as it is from the outside) has its charm.
Sentences	I have visited a number of nearby colleges. (I haven't decided on one yet.) However, I haven't been to Yale yet.
Numbers or Letters	The priorities in my schedule are (1) homework, (2) music practice, and (3) lifting weights.
Dates	Elizabeth Blackwell (1821–1910) was the first woman doctor.

The chart below illustrates the rules for punctuating and capitalizing material in parentheses. Notice, too, the punctuation outside the parentheses.

CAPITALIZATION AND PUNCTUATION WITH PARENTHESES	
Declarative Sentence	Andy (he'll be six in March) reads on a third-grade level.
Interrogative or Exclamatory Sentence	As soon as we got to the party (It was already mobbed!), the band began playing.
Sentence Between Sentences	I just got a letter from Marie Schmidt. (You remember her from softball.) She'll be visiting relatives in town next week.

▶ **Exercise 1** **Using Parentheses.** Add parentheses wherever they are appropriate.

EXAMPLE: On D-Day June 6, 1944 the Allied Forces landed at Normandy.
On D-Day (June 6, 1944) the Allied Forces landed at Normandy.

1. When the fire began sometime around 4:00 A.M., officials estimate, no one was in the building.

2. The honored guests were introduced in the following order: 1 Governor Hillyer, 2 Senator Parker, and 3 Mayor Goldberg.

3. Lee's surrender to Grant April 9, 1865 marked the end of the War Between the States.

4. Gretchen and Beatrix They are twins, aren't they? will be roommates next year.

▶ **Exercise 2** **More Work with Parentheses.** Rewrite each sentence adding parentheses as well as punctuation and capitalization where necessary.

EXAMPLE: Chris and Michelle aren't they your cousins left a message.
Chris and Michelle (Aren't they your cousins?) left a message.

1. Carol's house you should see the size of it is on a hill outside of town.

_____

2. Luciano Pavarotti born 1935 has achieved extraordinary popularity.

_____

3. Jen's party will you be there is sure to be fun.

_____

4. Mr. Porter he's the new superintendent of schools went to school with my mother.

_____

27.5 **Parentheses • Practice 2**

▶ **Exercise 1**   **Using Parentheses.**   Copy the following sentences, adding parentheses, any other punctuation marks, and capitals where necessary. Underline any words in italics.

EXAMPLE: Tickets for the play are hard to get it is a play I have wanted to see for a long time we finally were able to get some for next week.
   Tickets for the play are hard to get. (It is a play I have wanted to see for a long time.) We finally were able to get some for next week.

1. The shorter route it passes through the city and along a badly paved road will get you there in two hours.

   _____

2. The book *Washington Square* the film is called *The Heiress* describes Catherine Sloper's romance with Morris Townsend.

   _____

3. Marie collects stamps in these special categories: a animals and birds, b flowers, and c famous leaders.

   _____

4. The telephone number he left was 201 555-6701.

   _____

5. Harriet Beecher Stowe 1811–1896 lived to see her best-seller become a success on stage as well.

   _____

6. My brother do you think he will ever learn was late again.

   _____

7. The actor came to town we were amazed and gave us his autograph.

   _____

8. As she walked toward us using crutches not very gracefully she wished she had been more careful climbing the tree.

   _____

9. My alarm clock didn't go off possibly a power failure and I was late for school.

   _____

10. He returned he spent a year in Europe and joined his family's business.

   _____

▶ **Exercise 2**   **Using Parentheses.**   For each item, write a sentence in which you enclose the given information in parentheses.

EXAMPLE: about three o'clock
   We got to the party late (about three o'clock).

1. no one knew why

   _____

2. I couldn't believe it!

   _____

3. Have you heard?

   _____

4. 1922–1999

   _____

5. the one who is wearing a red sequined costume

   _____

Brackets • Practice 1

Brackets   Use brackets to enclose a word or words you insert in a quotation when you are quoting someone else. Brackets are also used sometimes with *sic* (thus) to show that the original writer misspelled a word or phrase.

USES OF BRACKETS	
Inserted Material	The author writes, "They [the Beatles] were the most influential rock band of the decade [the 1960's]."
With *sic*	He wrote, "I was extremely dismayed when I recieved [*sic*] the news."

▶ **Exercise 1**   **Using Brackets Correctly.**   Rewrite each sentence below, adding brackets to each.

EXAMPLE: The speaker continued: "It the Peace Corps attracted thousands of young people during the 1960's and '70's."

The speaker continued: "It [the Peace Corps] attracted thousands of young people during the 1960's and '70's."

1. She argued, many American citisens *sic* were angered by his the President's decision.

   _____

2. The author writes, "when he Coleridge published 'The Rime of the Ancient Mariner,' the Romantic Movement began."

   _____

3. "The novel The Young Visiters *sic* is my favorite," Susan began.

   _____

4. In the second chapter, the author writes, "Not satisfied with the celebrity of the silver screen, he Ronald Reagan entered politics."

   _____

5. Ellen's essay contained an interesting thesis: "As he Macbeth becomes stronger, she Lady Macbeth begins to decline."

   _____

▶ **Exercise 2**   **Using Dashes, Parentheses, and Brackets.**   Insert dashes, parentheses, or brackets in each sentence.

EXAMPLE: They the Giants won the game.
   They [the Giants] won the game.

1. That new rock video Are there any copies left in town? is super.

2. My little sister always asks for "bisgetti *sic* and meatballs."

3. Our new phone number is 203 555-1291.

4. The broadcaster reported where did he hear it? that a bomb had gone off.

5. At the news conference the President stated, "He the Secretary of State has issued a formal apology."

27.5 Brackets • Practice 2

▶ **Exercise 1**   **Using Brackets.**   In the following sentences, add brackets where necessary.

EXAMPLE: "The results of this vote 98–2 indicate overwhelming support for our proposal," he stated.
"The results of this vote [98–2] indicate overwhelming support for our proposal," he stated.

1. Her letter stated, "I recieved sic the order only yesterday."

2. Abraham Lincoln said: "We have come to dedicate a portion of that field the Gettysburg battlefield as a final resting place for those who here gave their lives that that nation might live."

3. Queen Elizabeth I once said, "God may forgive you the Countess of Nottingham, but I never can."

4. In his autobiography Moss Hart wrote, "The only credential the city New York asked was the boldness to dream."

5. Martin Luther King, Jr., stated his philosophy: "Let us not seek to satisfy our thirst for freedom by drinking from the cup of bitterness and hatred. He was speaking in Washington, D.C., in 1963. We must forever conduct our struggle on the high plane of dignity and discipline."

6. My little sister always says, "Me sic want to go with you."

7. My aunt sent us very exciting news: "We my aunt and uncle have decided to go to Alaska where we are planning to set up a salmon fishery."

8. The history teacher announced, "For tonight's assignment read about the war to end all wars World War I."

9. My little brother called, "Sister, Sister, turn sic here."

10. At the news conference, the spokesperson announced: "He the President will leave for Camp David tomorrow."

▶ **Writing Application**   **Using Dashes, Parentheses, and Brackets in Your Own Writing.**   Follow the directions for each of the following. Write your answers on a separate sheet of paper.

1. Write an original sentence using a dash to indicate an abrupt change of thought.

2. Write an original sentence using a dash to present a dramatic summary statement.

3. Use dashes in an original sentence to set off a nonessential appositive.

4. Use dashes in an original sentence to set off a nonessential modifier that contains punctuation.

5. Place a declarative sentence within parentheses within an original sentence.

6. Place a question within parentheses within a sentence.

7. Use parentheses to set off explanatory information involving numerals in an original sentence.

8. Use parentheses around numbers marking items in a series in an original sentence.

9. Place a declarative sentence within parentheses between two original sentences.

10. Use brackets correctly in an original sentence.

27.5 Hyphens • Practice 1

Use a hyphen when writing out numbers from twenty-one through ninety-nine and with fractions used as adjectives. Also use hyphens with certain prefixes and compound words and with compound modifiers before nouns (unless they are proper adjectives or contain an adverb ending in -ly).

USES OF HYPHENS		
With Numbers	thirty-nine steps	one-half cup
With Prefixes	pro-British	self-contained
With Compound Nouns	jack-in-the-box	mother-in-law
With Compound Modifiers	well-mannered child	best-dressed student
	friendly-looking dog	custom-built house

Using Hyphens at the Ends of Lines Divide words only between syllables. A word with a prefix or suffix can almost always be divided between the prefix and the root or the suffix and the root. Do not divide a word so that a single letter or the letters -ed stand alone. Divide hyphenated words only at the hyphen. Do not divide proper nouns or adjectives, and do not carry part of the word over to another page.

HYPHENS AT THE ENDS OF LINES				
Correct	straw-berry	be-long	ex-partner	Belgium
Incorrect	strawb-erry	a-long	ex-part-ner	Bel-gium

> **Exercise 1** **Using Hyphens.** Place hyphens where they are needed. (Not all sentences need hyphens.)

EXAMPLE: Paula has many far flung relatives.
　　　　　Paula has many far-flung relatives.

1. It is not uncommon for a two year old to have tantrums.

2. Jimmy stared at the lights in wide eyed wonder.

3. Of the case of soda bottles, twenty two were the wrong kind.

4. The bill passed by a three fourths majority.

5. That is an oddly shaped package.

6. The solution seemed self evident.

7. Several pro Russian journalists were asked to leave the meeting.

8. Eleanor gave a first rate performance.

9. Do you have any up to date information on the flood conditions?

10. Thirty eight more members have joined in the last half hour.

> **Exercise 2** **Hyphenating Words.** Rewrite each word below, using a hyphen at any place where the word could be divided at the end of a line of writing.

EXAMPLE: examine ___*ex-am-ine*___ prayers ___*prayers*___

1. perjury _____
2. Israeli _____
3. rhymes _____
4. self-fulfilling _____
5. profound _____

6. inform _____
7. elastic _____
8. length _____
9. different _____
10. decide _____

27.5 Hyphens • Practice 2

Exercise 1   **Using Hyphens to Combine Words.**   In each of the following items, add hyphens where necessary. If an item does not require a hyphen, write *correct*.

EXAMPLE: Chinese speaking guest
Chinese-speaking guest

1. well educated person _____
2. greatly admired _____
3. twenty three years _____
4. un American action _____
5. self satisfied man _____
6. South American custom _____
7. well made chair _____
8. all American athlete _____
9. treasurer elect _____
10. father in law _____
11. anti war speech _____
12. semi independent act _____
13. T shirt _____
14. bright eyed child _____
15. ex lieutenant _____
16. pre Revolutionary _____
17. old fashioned dress _____
18. L shaped building _____
19. one hundredth part _____
20. multi colored fabric _____

Exercise 2   **Using Hyphens to Divide Words at the Ends of Lines.**   If a word has been divided as it should be if it appeared at the end of a line, write *correct*. If it has been divided incorrectly, write the word as it should appear.

EXAMPLE: dre-am   *dream*

1. Anglo-Ameri-can _____
2. a-lone _____
3. thro-ugh _____
4. Pe-ter _____
5. Syl-via _____
6. si-xteen _____
7. i-dea _____
8. guilt-y _____
9. Span-ish _____
10. self-in-terest _____

27.5 # Apostrophes With Possessives • Practice 1

Forming Possessives of Nouns   Use the following rules to form possessive nouns.

FORMING POSSESSIVE NOUNS	
Add an apostrophe and an -s to most singular nouns.	that tree's fruit Mr. Hooper's store
Add just an apostrophe to plural nouns ending in -s.	those trees' fruit the Hoopers' neighbor
Add an apostrophe and an -s to plural nouns that do not end in -s.	the geese's formation the children's toys
Make the last word in a compound noun possessive.	my sister-in-law's cooking the passer-by's expression
Treat time, amounts, and the word *sake* like other possessives.	fifty cents' worth, an hour's wait, for Tim's sake, for the boys' sake
To show individual ownership, make each noun in the series possessive.	Ann's and Sue's clothes the boys' and girls' bicycles
To show joint ownership, make the last noun in the series possessive.	Ann and Sue's parents the boys and girls' interest

Forming Possessives of Pronouns   Use an apostrophe and an -s with indefinite pronouns to show possession. Do not use an apostrophe with the possessive forms of personal pronouns.

POSSESSIVE FORMS OF PRONOUNS		
Indefinite		**Personal**
anyone's	one anothers'	my, mine, our, ours, your, yours
nobody's	each other's	his, her, hers, its, their, theirs

▶ **Exercise 1**   **Writing Possessive Forms of Nouns.**   Write the possessive form on the line.

EXAMPLE: within the throw of a stone _____*within a stone's throw*_____

1. the tip for the waitress _____

2. the pen name of Charles Dodgson _____

3. the test scores of Howard and Bill _____

4. for the sake of the neighbors _____

5. a cruise for six weeks _____

▶ **Exercise 2**   **Writing Possessive Forms of Pronouns.**   In each blank, write the correct possessive form for the pronoun in parentheses.

EXAMPLE: Are these gloves _____*yours*_____?   (you)

1. By mistake I grabbed _____ sweater.   (someone else)

2. The puppy chewed through _____ leash.   (it)

3. Shall we have the party at your house or at _____?   (they)

4. The two sisters sometimes borrow _____ clothes.   (each other)

27.5 Apostrophes With Possessives • Practice 2

▶ **Exercise 1** **Using Apostrophes Correctly to Form Possessive Nouns.** In each of the following
sentences, underline the correct possessive form.

EXAMPLE: I bought five (dollar's, <u>dollars'</u>) worth of stamps.

1. My (mother's-in-law, mother-in-law's) baked scampi won a prize in a local contest.
2. He loaded the (women's, womens') luggage into the bus.
3. Some of (Dolores', Dolores's) friends are coming for dinner.
4. Is this really the (Joneses', Jones's) house?
5. The (boy's, boys') parents gave the boys permission.
6. (Margie and Trish's, Margie's and Trish's) projects both received outstanding grades.
7. All of the reporters were asked to read the (editor's-in-chief, editor-in-chief's) style sheet.
8. We need one (hour's, hours') worth of your time.
9. I've always been interested in (children's, childrens') art work.
10. An (electrician's, electricians') tools must be cared for.

▶ **Exercise 2** **Using Apostrophes Correctly with Pronouns.** In each of the following sentences,
underline the correct form from the choices in parentheses.

EXAMPLE: I need (<u>somebody else's</u>, somebody elses') opinion.

1. This chemistry notebook obviously belongs to (her's, her).
2. (Someone else's, Someone elses') car was hit, not mine.
3. (Whose, Who's) briefcase is on the table?
4. Susan found (someones', someone's) social security card.
5. Our cat always eats (it's, its) meal in the broom closet.
6. They visited (each others', each other's) houses often.
7. Our new neighbor's pool is larger than (their's, theirs).
8. I wonder what happened to (he's, his) report card.
9. I originally wanted to use (they're, their) lawn mower.
10. (Everybody's, Everybodys') attendance is requested.

27.6 Apostrophes: Contractions and Special Situations • Practice 1

Forming Contractions Use an apostrophe in a contraction to indicate the position of the missing letter or letters.

COMMON CONTRACTIONS			
Verbs with Not	shouldn't (should not)	isn't (is not)	won't (will not)
Pronouns with Verbs	he'll (he will)	you'll (you will)	they'll (they will)
	she'd (she would)	you'd (you would)	we'd (we would)
	I've (I have)	you've (you have)	they've (they have)
	I'm (I am)	you're (you are)	we're (we are)
Other Kinds of Contractions	class of '88	o'er	
	o'clock	goin'	

Using Apostrophes in Special Situations Use an apostrophe and an -s to write the plurals of numbers, symbols, letters, and words used to name themselves.

APOSTROPHES USED IN SPECIAL SITUATIONS
Use *'s to indicate footnoted material. Young children often mistake *b*'s and *d*'s.

▶ **Exercise 1** **Writing Contractions.** Make contractions from the word(s) in parentheses to complete each sentence.

EXAMPLE: _____*I'd*_____ rather not go to that party.   (I would)

1. _____ be ready in a minute.   (We will)

2. We _____ expect too much more help from Teddy.   (cannot)

3. _____ been waiting for your call.   (She has)

4. Mr. Harper has the reputation of being a _____ -do-well.   (never)

5. I hope _____ pleased with her gift.   (she is)

6. These pictures _____ the ones we took on vacation.   (are not)

7. We will leave promptly at six _____ .   (of the clock)

8. My sister graduated from college in _____ .   (1984)

9. Wally's parents _____ let him go camping with us.   (will not)

10. _____ been waiting for that bus for an hour.   (They have)

▶ **Exercise 2** **Using Apostrophes Correctly.** Rewrite each sentence below, adding apostrophes where they are needed.

EXAMPLE: Someone had doodled $s all over the phone message.
_____*Someone had doodled $'s all over the phone message.*_____

1. Angie's *os* and *as* look very much alike.

   _____

2. When you review your essay, try to eliminate some of the *ands*.

   _____

3. Tom adds some peculiar flourishes to his *Ts*.

   _____

4. That little boy writes his *9s* backwards.

   _____

5. Grandma always tells us to mind our *ps* and *qs*.

   _____

27.6 Apostrophes: Contractions and Special Situations • Practice 2

▶ **Exercise 1**   **Using Apostrophes in Contractions.**   Write the contraction for each of the following items.

EXAMPLE: should not ____*shouldn't*____

1. we have _____
2. who is _____
3. would not _____
4. 1981 _____
5. it is _____

6. they are _____
7. will not _____
8. of the clock _____
9. I am _____
10. over _____

▶ **Exercise 2**   **Using Apostrophes in Special Situations.**   Write the plural form of each of the following items. Underline all words in italics.

EXAMPLE: if ____*if's*____

1. 1980 _____
2. *and* _____
3. *C* _____
4. 1930 _____
5. *6* _____

6. *but* _____
7. *!* _____
8. *i* _____
9. *2* _____
10. *?* _____

▶ **Writing Application**   **Using Apostrophes in Your Own Writing.**   Write a sentence for each of the following items.

1. Use the possessive case to show joint ownership of a horse.

_____

2. Use the possessive case to indicate a book owned by Charles.

_____

3. Use the possessive case to indicate a house owned by a family named Jones.

_____

4. Use the possessive case to show individual ownership of shoes belonging to Maria and Louise.

_____

5. Use the possessive case to indicate a baseball bat owned by Arthur.

_____

6. Use the possessive case to indicate a lawn mower owned by your brother-in-law.

_____

7. Use the possessive form of a personal pronoun to show ownership of a notebook.

_____

8. Use the possessive form of an indefinite pronoun to show ownership of a pen.

_____

9. Use the contraction of *who is.*

_____

10. Use the plural of the word *however* used to name itself.

_____

Diagraming Subjects, Verbs, and Modifiers
• Practice 1

Subjects, Verbs, and Modifiers   In a sentence diagram, the subject and the verb are written on a horizontal line with the subject on the left and the verb on the right. A vertical line separates the subject and verb. Adjectives and adverbs are placed on slanted lines directly below the words they modify.

SUBJECT AND VERB
Karen will be going.

Karen	will be going

ADDING ADJECTIVES AND ADVERBS
The large brown dog barked very loudly.

▶ **Exercise 1**   **Diagraming Subjects and Verbs, Adjectives and Adverbs.**   Correctly diagram each sentence. Refer to the examples above if you need to.

1. The hockey players grinned happily.

2. The angry wrestlers sneered menacingly.

3. A young man lives here.

▶ **Exercise 2**   **More Work with Diagrams.**   Correctly diagram each sentence.

1. The pretty red balloon floated up.

2. Her overly ambitious plans were quickly rejected.

Diagraming Subjects, Verbs, and Modifiers
• Practice 2

Exercise 1   **Diagraming Subjects, Verbs, and Modifiers.**   Correctly diagram each sentence.

1. Susan studies hard.

2. The young deer bounded away.

3. Many heavy snowfalls occurred last winter.

4. Bob, quit now.

5. Have the people left already?

Diagraming With Conjunctions • **Practice 1**

Adding Conjunctions In a diagram, a conjunction is written on a dotted line drawn between the words that it connects.

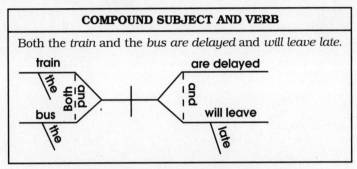

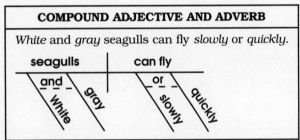

▷ **Exercise 1** **Diagraming Sentences with Conjunctions.** Correctly diagram each sentence.

1. The book and the dictionary are there.

2. The little girl often laughs but sometimes cries.

3. The deer moved gracefully and swiftly.

▷ **Exercise 2** **More Work with Conjunctions.** Correctly diagram each sentence.

1. Both his car and his boat were stolen.

2. The Republicans and Democrats debated and argued tirelessly.

Diagraming With Conjunctions • Practice 2

1. The yellow roses and the pink impatiens are blooming profusely.

2. The tractor moved slowly but steadily.

3. The big, gleaming jetliner is now taxiing.

4. The old automobile sputtered and stalled.

5. The young actress was enthusiastically smiling and waving.

6. Wendy sings and dances beautifully.

7. The homework was difficult but interesting.

8. Joe, Rachel, and Frank are moving.

Diagraming Complements • Practice 1

Complements   Place a direct object on the main horizontal line after the verb. The direct object is separated from the verb with a short vertical line. Place an indirect object under the verb on a short horizontal line extending from a slanted line. An objective complement is placed next to the direct object and separated from it with a slanted line.

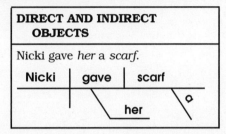

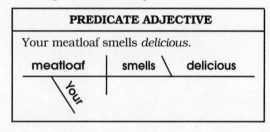

Predicate nominatives and predicate adjectives are diagramed the same way. Place them on the main line after the verb and separate them from the verb with a line slanting toward the subject.

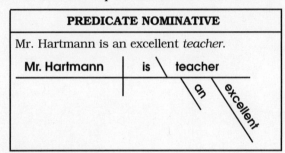

▶ **Exercise 1**   **Diagraming Sentences with Complements.**   Correctly diagram each sentence.

1. You can paint the silo red.

2. Your last sketch is beautiful.

3. I brought the boys an unusual souvenir.

▶ **Exercise 2**   **More Work with Complements.**   Correctly diagram each sentence.

1. The President is an effective negotiator.

2. Mom gave Aunt Elvira a strange look.

Diagraming Complements • Practice 2

Diagraming Complements. Correctly diagram each sentence.

1. Carol and Phyllis are playing chess.

2. Mr. Connors skillfully repaired a camera and a CD player.

3. The young girl wrote her friend a lengthy note.

4. The construction workers seemed both confident and energetic.

5. The film critic labeled the new movie both very exciting and emotionally gripping.

Diagraming Sentences With Prepositional Phrases • Practice 1

Prepositional Phrases   A prepositional phrase is diagramed directly beneath the word it modifies. The preposition goes on a slanted line and the object sits on a horizontal line. If a prepositional phrase modifies the object of a preposition in another phrase, it is diagramed directly under the object of the preposition of the first phrase. If it modifies an adverb it is connected directly to the adverb.

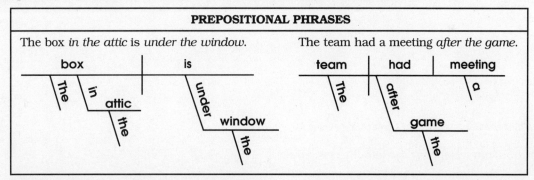

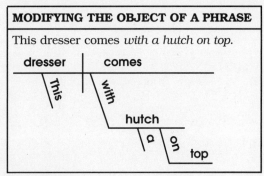
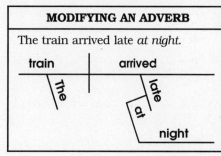

▶ **Exercise 1**   **Diagraming Prepositional Phrases.**   Diagram the following sentences. Refer to the models above if necessary.

1. The closet in the hall is full.

2. She ate breakfast in the kitchen.

▶ **Exercise 2**   **More Diagraming.**   Diagram the following sentences.

1. These jeans come with starbursts on the pockets.

2. The dancers appeared early on the program.

Diagraming Sentences With Prepositional Phrases • Practice 2

▶ **Exercise 1** **Diagraming Prepositional Phrases.** Correctly diagram each sentence.

1. The bridge over the river contains many tons of steel.

2. Tomorrow, I am moving my car into the new garage.

3. The volcano spewed ash onto the forest below the peak.

4. The railroad tracks snake along the river and dash into the tunnel.

5. Betty purchased the new aviation stamps and added them to her collection.

Diagraming Sentences With Appositive Phrases • Practice 1

Appositive Phrases   Place an appositive in parentheses beside the noun or pronoun it renames. Position any modifiers of the appositive in the usual way beneath the appositive.

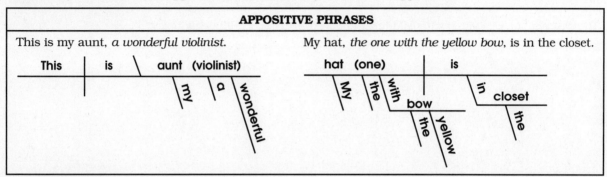

▷ **Exercise 1**   **Diagraming Sentences with Appositive Phrases.**   In the spaces provided below, diagram the following sentences.

1. I enjoyed the music, a series of marches.

2. That car, the one with a color television, is too expensive.

▷ **Exercise 2**   **More Diagraming.**   Correctly diagram each sentence.

1. The pitcher, a tall, thin lefthander, took the mound.

2. I bought a new timepiece, a gold watch from Switzerland.

Diagraming Sentences With Appositive Phrases • Practice 2

▶ **Exercise 1** **Diagraming Appositive Phrases.** Correctly diagram each sentence.

1. The new pet, a perky kitten with gold fur, gladdened the hearts of the children.

2. At the meeting, each member received new membership cards, gold ones with black lettering.

3. His teacher, Mr. Tambro, plays chess very well.

4. The company gave Ms. Kelly, a brilliant computer expert, a well-deserved promotion.

5. The park ranger observed the animals, a herd of elk, in the meadow.

Diagraming Sentences With Verbal Phrases
• Practice 1

Verbal Phrases   A participle is placed partly on a slanted line and partly on a horizontal line beneath the noun or pronoun it modifies. Complements are placed on the horizontal line after the participle, set off with a short vertical rule.

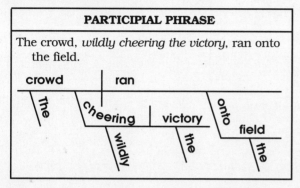

PARTICIPIAL PHRASE

The crowd, *wildly cheering the victory*, ran onto the field.

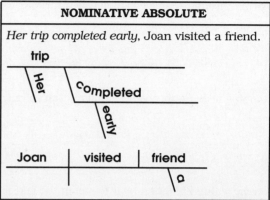

NOMINATIVE ABSOLUTE

Her trip completed early, Joan visited a friend.

Gerunds and gerund phrases used as subjects, direct objects, or predicate nominatives are placed atop a pedestal. When a gerund or gerund phrase is used as an indirect object or object of a preposition, the stepped line extends from a slanted line. An infinitive used as a noun is diagramed on a pedestal. When an infinitive acts as an adjective or an adverb, its diagram is similar to that of a prepositional phrase. If an infinitive has an understood *to*, add it to the diagram in parentheses.

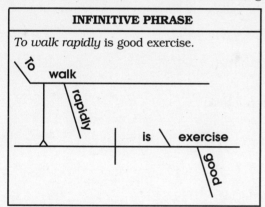

INFINITIVE PHRASE

To walk rapidly is good exercise.

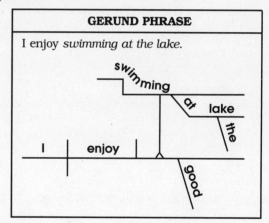

GERUND PHRASE

I enjoy *swimming at the lake*.

▶ **Exercise 1**   **Diagraming Verbal Phrases.**   In the spaces provided below, diagram the sentences.

1. I like dancing in the moonlight.

2. I know the road to take to the park.

Diagraming Sentences With Verbal Phrases
• Practice 2

▶ **Exercise 1** **Diagraming Verbal Phrases.** Correctly diagram each sentence.

1. Driving through the new tunnel was a thrilling experience.

2. Jumping in her crib, the little child began to laugh at all of us.

3. Jeremy wanted to find a boat to sail in the lake.

4. The remnants of the birthday party, dirty dishes piled in the sink, were surveyed by my father.

5. Preserving natural wonders for future generations is a difficult task.

6. Her goal, to attend a fine university, will require much sacrificing.

▶ **Exercise 2** **More Diagraming.** Correctly diagram each sentence.

1. The girl chosen for the team is my sister.

2. His confidence destroyed, he resigned from his job.

Diagraming Compound Sentences • Practice 1

Compound Sentences   Diagram each independent clause of a compound sentence as you would a separate sentence. Then, join the verbs of the clauses with a dotted step line. On the step line, write either the coordinating conjunction or the semicolon that joins the two clauses.

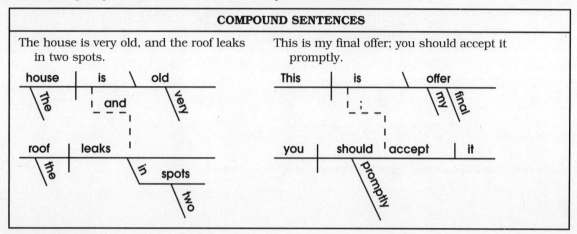

> **Exercise 1**   **Diagraming Compound Sentences.**   In the spaces provided, diagram the sentences below.

1. I understand your problems fully, and I sympathize with you.

2. I will drive to the station; you must remain at home.

> **Exercise 2**   **More Diagraming.**   Correctly diagram each sentence.

1. Sara will prepare the fruit; Bob will buy an appetizer for the meal.

2. The road has been repaired, so you should be able to reach the bridge.

Diagraming Compound Sentences • Practice 2

▶ **Exercise 1**   **Diagraming Compound Sentences.**   Diagram the following compound sentences.

1. His car skidded in the snow, but Mr. Burns continued to drive many more miles.

2. The rain had cooled the air but, by late afternoon, the heat returned.

3. Did William eat his lunch, or did he save the sandwiches for a later time?

4. Last January was cold, but February was even colder.

5. The wolves howled at the moon, and the campers cowered in their tents.

Diagraming Complex Sentences • Practice 1

Complex Sentences   Both adjective and adverb clauses are diagramed on a line beneath the independent clause and connected to the independent clause by a dotted line. With an adjective clause, the dotted line extends from the noun or pronoun the clause modifies to the relative pronoun or relative adverb in the clause. With an adverb clause, the dotted line extends from the word modified to the verb in the adverb clause. The subordinate conjunction is written along the dotted line.

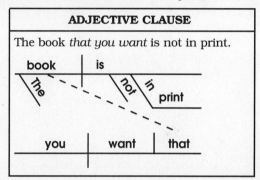

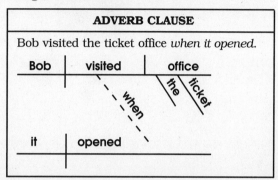

A noun clause is placed on a pedestal extending upward from the position it fills in the independent clause. If the introductory word has no function in the noun clause, it is written along the pedestal.

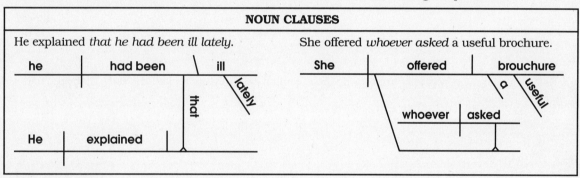

▷ **Exercise 1**   **Diagraming Complex Sentences.**   Diagram the following sentences.

1. Sue will drive to Dayton if we ask her.

2. I know that my friends will volunteer.

▷ **Exercise 2**   **More Diagraming.**   Correctly diagram each sentence.

1. We gave whoever reported a list of activities.

2. We have a new dictionary that you may like.

Diagraming Complex Sentences • Practice 2

▶ **Exercise 1**   **Diagraming Complex Sentences.**   Diagram the following complex sentences.

1. Ms. Lopez, who conducts scientific research, will supervise the project for us.

2. We must do whatever is needed to achieve our goal.

3. Because the experiment was very important, the chemists carefully rechecked the data that they had recorded.

4. When you purchase a new appliance, check for any defects in its parts.

5. The rains finally fell, although many people had abandoned their farms by then.

Diagraming Compound-Complex Sentences
• Practice 1

Compound-Complex Sentences   To diagram a compound-complex sentence, begin by diagraming each of the independent clauses. Then diagram the subordinate clause(s).

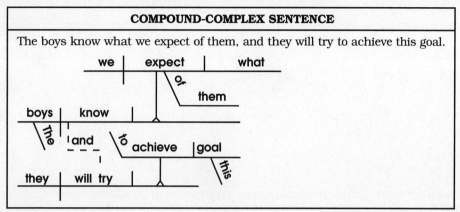

COMPOUND-COMPLEX SENTENCE

The boys know what we expect of them, and they will try to achieve this goal.

▶ **Exercise 1**   **Diagraming Compound-Complex Sentences.**   Diagram the following sentences.

1.   How we play today is important; it will have a major effect on the rest of our season.

2.   We have received nothing from her since she left, and we have begun to worry.

▶ **Exercise 2**   **Diagraming Sentences of Varying Structures.**   Identify the structure of each sentence and diagram it correctly. The sentences may be compound, complex, or compound-complex.

1.   This is the road that leads to Mount Vernon.

2.   I reached the game late, but I got a seat.

3.   If you can recommend a good restaurant, I would appreciate it.

4.   I can tell how her mind works, and I am afraid of what she might do.

Diagraming Compound-Complex Sentences
• Practice 2

▶ **Exercise 1**   **Diagraming Compound-Complex Sentences.**   Diagram the following
compound-complex sentences.

1. While we watched the approaching train, the locomotive loomed larger, and the engineer sounded the
   horn.

2. He left the house before the light of dawn appeared, but by evening he still continued to do more
   work.

3. If we visit the farm, I want to pick some corn, and my brother plans to feed the chickens.

4. As the storm increased in force, Ivan crawled under the bed, and Hillary covered her head with a
   pillow.

5. I knew immediately that I had made a mistake, but I was ashamed to admit it.